CASE MANAGEMENT:

HISTORICAL

CURRENT

& FUTURE

PERSPECTIVES

Edited by Mary Hubbard Linz,
Patricia McAnally, and Colleen Wieck

Foreword by Professor Ro
Director, Minnesota University
on Developmental Di

D1227295

**BROOKLINE
BOOKS**

Library of Congress Cataloging-in-Publication Data

Case management : historical, current, and future perspectives/
   edited by Mary Hubbard Linz, Patricia McAnally, Colleen Wieck.
     p. cm.
   Papers Presented at a Conference co-sponsored by the Minnesota University Affiliated Program on Developmental Disabilities and the Minnesota Dept. of Human Service, held in 1986.
   Includes bibliographical references.
   ISBN 0-914797-65-4 : $24.95
   1. Developmentally disabled--Service for--United States-
-Management--Congress. 2. Social case work--United States-
-Management--Congress. I. Linz, Mary Hubbard. II. McAnally, Patricia L., 1927-   . III. Wieck, Colleen A. (Colleen Ann)
IV. Minnesota University Affiliated Program on Developmental Disabilities. V. Minnesota. Dept. of Human Services.
HV1570.5.U65C37 1989
362.1'968--dc20

       89-23917
       CIP

Published by
Brookline Books, Inc.
PO Box 1046
Cambridge, MA 02238-1046

Printed in the United States of America

Preface

*When we try to pick out anything by itself, we find it
hitched to everything else in the universe.*
John Muir

Approximately 25 years ago, a noted attorney titled a perceptive article on the challenges facing society and contemporary educational institutions, "Everything Nailed Down is Coming Up Loose" (Fishwick, 1963). This expression, taken from a different context, aptly describes much of the current condition of services today for citizens with disabilities and their families. Despite enormous gains in funding and more enlightened attitudes in many countries, services to citizens with disabilities are still managed through an incredibly complex maze of legal guidelines and archaic management strategies at every level of government. Recognition of this longstanding problem has consumed the attention of numerous conferences and the pages of extensive reports for much of the past 20 years. Yet, many of our structures and strategies in providing human services have changed little during this period. In fact, they continue to function with little coordination, efficiency, or effectiveness at a time when integration of purpose and action are urgently required to address the service needs of people with disabilities and their family members.

It is true that life experiences of most people with disabilities have changed in the past few decades. These changes reflect increased concern in many countries for expanding opportunity, integration, and equity for all citizens. For citizens with disabilities and their families, social advances have been reflected in a changing, more progressive philosophy toward integration in education, residential living, employment, and community participation. Such changes have increased recognition and extension of their legal rights and substantially increased public support for education, residential living, income maintenance, training, and other essential services in communities as opposed to segregated institutional service models.

Progressive social changes are often attended by unintended problems and consequences. Despite positive growth in opportunity and acceptance of citizens with disabilities, difficult problems are still evident in programs and supports available to them. With the decentralization of services from more segregated service models, attempts to increase the social integration and family support for people with disabilities have been thwarted by increasing fragmentation of responsibility among many varied agencies. The profound changes in service programs, through decentralization, reduced size, and other changes clearly have not been matched by improved access or in the quality and effectiveness of interventions. Progress of the past few decades, moreover, has not been without the intense conflict over purpose and strategy which invariably accompanies any dramatic social change or change in public policy and practices.

There are still many important challenges ahead in improving access, appropriateness, efficiency, coordination and accountability of services, and supports for people with disabilities. Much of the success of past and current reform in services and programs of support will depend upon the success of case management strategies, particularly in local communities. This important book addresses this essential, but too often ignored, ingredient to assuring full opportunity, inclusion, and citizenship for persons with disabilities.

The term *case management* enjoys many different definitions and interpretations. As community-centered services and support programs have evolved, however, the concept has clearly expanded to address a wide range of issues including strategies necessary to *ensure access and equity*; planning involving persons with disabilities, family members, providers, and others; *coordination* of effort and resources; and *assurance* of appropriateness, efficiency, and quality in services and programs of support. Sound case management practices should produce better planning and coordination of programs, but it should also be concerned with increasing the quality of life for people with disabilities in the communities in which they live, learn, and work.

In an area with limited literature and research, *Case Management: Historical, Current, and Future Perspectives*, explores this important issue from multiple perspectives. It emphasizes major historical, functional, and conceptual issues, the life cycle needs of persons with disabilities and their families, the essential importance of organizing the natural strengths of communities, the creative roles of parents and other family members, new and creative case management models, the implications of critical life transitions in early childhood and later adolescence, and important challenges in philosophy, law, regulation, and management practices in providing support through case management. Above all, this book is about improving the connections of people with needed support and services with their friends and with their communities.

This book contains essential material and concepts for addressing the role of case management in the many and varied challenges of providing full opportunity for citizens with disabilities in our homes, schools, and communities. Effective case management strategies increasingly serve as the catalyst and guarantor of reform in practices. They help to assure greater effectiveness in services and programs of support in local communities.

This book addresses the many challenging aspects of case management, arguing for a perspective on community living and integration in which service coordination is a broadly shared responsibility and process involving the coordination and participation of families, persons with disabilities, local and state government organizations, and service providers. Written with a multidisciplinary perspective, this book is an important source for students, policy makers, researchers, local managers, providers, and family members. It is essential reading for anyone who cares about the direction and success of strategies to assure a better quality of life and opportunity for persons with disabilities.

ROBERT H. BRUININKS, PH.D.
Institute on Community Integration
University of Minnesota
Minneapolis, Minnesota
March, 1990

Foreward

In 1986, a conference was held in Minnesota to address topics in case management for persons with developmental disabliltiies. This conference was co-sponsored by the Minnesota University Affiliated Program for Persons with Developmental Disabilities and the Minnesota Department of Human Services. At that time, several conference speakers gave their consent for the publication of their presentations (McKnight, Bergman, McDonald, Pendler). Other chapters were solicited from experts in the field (Lipsky, Wieck, Wray, Granquist). We sought to combine historical discussion of case management with discussion of current practices, and of future trends, as well, using the expertise of both personnel and parents involved in the field of case management. We hope that readers will be pleased with the breadth of the discussion of case management found in this volume.

Mary Hubbard Linz, Ph.D.
University of Minnesota, UAP

Table of Contents

CHAPTER I

Research Review of Effectiveness of Case Management in the United States

by Angela Novak Amado, Patricia L. McAnally, and Mary Hubbard Linz

T he evolution of case management has its roots in the development of professionalized social work and publicly-funded human services. Research on the effectiveness of case management is also based in research exploring the effectiveness of social work practices and in evaluation studies of existing case management systems. In this chapter, the historical development of case management is reviewed, including how it differs from traditional social work and its evolution through federal laws and guidelines. Empirical research on the effectiveness of case management systems and of case management practices is also reviewed. Summaries of previous evaluations of statewide case management systems in other states and in Minnesota conclude this section.

History of Case Management

As early as the 19th century, charitable organizations were providing services to persons who were poor and needy, an undertaking which predated any organized government role in the delivery of human services. The current delivery of human services is derived from the fragmented and duplicative efforts of these early, singular organizations. During the intervening years, agencies have struggled with the development of comprehensive and unified strategies for delivering services.

A significant impact in the development of organized services occurred with the Social Security Act of 1932. In addition to establishing a major role for the federal government in meeting human needs, the Social Security Act also attempted to bring together several different categorical programs (e.g., public assistance, social insurance maternal and child health) in a logical relationship (Rice, 1977).

The next great wave of federal legislation for social services, occurring in the 1960s, moved toward coordinating services, focusing on existing and newly formed resources in a systematized approach to target problems. Numerous problem- centered legislative actions, such as the Mental Health Act, Comprehensive Health Services Act, Office of Economic Opportunity, and Model Cities legislation attempted to bring together previously separated programs in medicine, welfare, mental health, and planning to function in harmony (Rice, 1977).

However, the swell of Federal initiatives in the 1960s led to the development of a large number of separately established social service agencies in the 1970s which were organized around the concept of a single service or set of services. The result was a service delivery system specialized and compartmentalized into separate bureaucracies in such diverse areas as vocational rehabilitation, mental health, child welfare, and developmental disabilities.

In 1962, the President's Panel on Mental Retardation expressed concern for the effectiveness with which consumers could secure needed services, and proposed the "continuum of care" as a critical consideration for service system planners. In response to strong advocacy for alternatives to institutionalization, many of these concepts suggested in "A Proposed Program for National Action to Combat Mental Retardation" (President's Panel on Mental Retardation, 1962) would later evolve into what is now called case management.

The mixed success of the social services programs in the 1960s led to efforts to place many services into one coordinated administrative stream. The relative explosion in human services initiated in the 1960's "Kennedy era" gave rise to numerous programs, criticisms of those programs, and strategies for improving services. As a result, critical attempts were made to establish programs that would integrate services, and these programs became the fore-runners of case management.

The term "services integration" was coined to describe federally initiated activities which attempted to build linkages among human service programs and bring coordination to the social service system. In 1971, the Secretary of Health, Education and Welfare, Elliot Richardson, declared services integration as a policy objective in a memorandum entitled "Services Integration: Next Steps." The objectives of services integration programs were: (a) the coordinated delivery of services for the greatest benefit to the people, (b) a holistic approach to the individual family unit, (c) the provision of a comprehensive range of services locally, and (d) the rational allocation of resources at the local level to be responsive to local needs (Richardson, 1971).

That year, 45 pilot demonstration projects called the Services Integration Targets of Opportunity (SITO) were initiated to establish new state or local interagency linkages. Under these grants, numerous techniques were developed and demonstrated including client tracking systems, information and referral systems, interagency planning and service delivery agreements, computerized resource inventories, and management reorganization projects (Mittenthal, 1975). Although some SITO projects were successful, some were unsuccessful. This was due to such factors as: a history of elaborate designs that were never implemented, resistance from local categorical programs, and withdrawal of federal research and development funds after the three-year pilot program (John, 1976).

For persons with developmental disabilities, Intagliata (1981) has postulated that the pressing need for case management has emerged in response to two major forces that have radically altered the human services environment over the last two decades. The first was the rapid expansion of human service programs that erupted throughout the sixties and into the early seventies. As a consequence of this expansion, the overall availability of services increased, although categorically, leading to the complex, fragmented, duplicate, and uncoordinated system currently available (Wray & Wieck, 1985). Deficiencies of the service system have proliferated in the evaluation literature in consistent references to "system overlap," "system duplication," "fragmented system" and "clients falling between the cracks" (Caragonne, 1984). A number of studies in the 1970s showed that services provided to persons with handicaps and their families were complex, uncoordinated, and confusing to those who needed them most and who most needed easy access to them (Kakalik et al., 1973; Office of Management and Budget, 1978). Randolph, Spurrier and Abramczyk (1981) found that the person with a developmental disability, in particular, runs the risk of being one of the most poorly served of social service clients. In addition, judicial attention began to play a major role in the development of services. In 1977 in the major litigation of *Halderman v. Pennhurst*, the federal district court found that "lack of accountability in case management was the central reason for the lack of movement from institution to the community" (Laski & Spitalnik, 1979, p. 1).

The second force that radically changed the human services system and contributed to the importance of case management was the deinstitutionalization movement. Moving from the "under one roof" model of services provided in the institution to the diffused care and support system in the community brought about a different set of significant problems. The negative consequences of the failure to provide adequate and appropriate community care to deinstitutionalized persons received widespread attention in the 1970s (Bassuk & Gerson, 1978; GAO Report, 1976; Lamb & Goertzel, 1971; Segal & Aviram, 1978; Willer, Scheerenberger & Intagliata, 1978). By the end of the 1970s, the need for case management to improve coordination of services was, again, the focus of renewed attention in human service programs. This focus was in response to various federal mandates in different laws regarding human services and was partly a function of many positive evaluation reports detailing the benefits derived from the use of case managers (Gans & Horton, 1975). During the 1970s, it also became evident that the mental health deinstitutionalization programs had led to many persons with mental health problems being "dumped" in the community without sufficient support. The National Institute of Mental Health proposed a comprehensive network of services, a coordinated community support system for such persons, with the key element being case management as the mechanism for coordinating all system efforts (Rice, 1977). In these community support programs, the case manager was designated as having case coordination responsibility within existing community resource networks.

Efforts by professionals, consumers, and advocates for persons with developmental disabilities also continued into the 1970s, resulting in federal support monies and federal and state legislation which encouraged the development of services to meet the individual needs of each client. Congress passed the first Developmental Disabilities Act in 1974 which specifically identified case management as a priority service component. The Developmental Disabilities Assistance and Bill of Rights Act (P.L. 95-602) included a requirement that each state receiving federal monies for developmental disabilities would allocate a substantial portion of its federal funds under the Act to at least one of four priority services. "Case management" was among them and remained a priority service in the Developmental Disabilities Assistance and Bill of Rights Act of 1984. As a result of the "priority service" requirement, there has been an increased need for information about case management and guidance in planning for its implementation under different circumstances. Many individual states began to enact legislation regarding case management that complemented the federal action in the late 1970s and early 1980s. In 1981, the Minnesota legislature passed amendments to Minnesota Statutes (Section 256E.08, Subdivision 1), which established a basic framework for the functions of case managers in the state.

With the proliferation and the increased cost of services, the complexity of the service system multiplied for all types of persons with disabilities requiring long-term care. In each of the fields addressing persons with long-term care needs, some strategy regarding coordination of services has evolved and has included case management. Potentially large deficits in state Medicaid budgets for long-term care have also forced many state budget personnel, human services, and Medicaid directors to seek ways to control costs. Sufficient evidence exists regarding cost reduction possibilities with coordinated community services and alternatives to institutionalization, to move vigorously toward the development of these alternatives. Hence, case management has been viewed as a key element in cost control (Simpson, 1982).

In services for elderly persons with health problems, case management has increasingly become a critical factor (Simpson, 1982). Given that chronic illness affects more than 80% of the elderly in the country, these persons are proportionally greater consumers of the nation's health care services. This increasing demand for health care services has created a crisis in health care delivery along with a crisis of enormously increasing Medicaid expenditures for nursing home care for elderly citizens. Many states (e.g., Wisconsin, New York, Virginia, and Minnesota) have developed community care programs encouraging elderly persons to remain at home as long as possible. Case management has been included as a necessary component of these programs, which have in some cases included persons with disabilities as well as senior citizens. Several studies have indicated that in this type of coordinated care, case management can make a difference in public costs. Seidl, Applebaum, Austin, and Mahoney (1983) showed two key results in a rigorously controlled random sample study in Wisconsin focused on systematized case management for long-term care clients. One finding was that appropriate community care was at least no more costly than nursing home care, even with all the administrative and start-up costs involved in the development of the community care services. Secondly, one of the key factors in keeping health care costs at a minimum was that case managers played a primary role in significantly reducing emergency room visits.

This type of coordinated approach to care has also been adopted from the long-term care field to health services for the general population. Given the rising costs of health care in all areas, health maintenance organizations (HMOs) and coordinated health plans have incorporated the concept of unifying services with one deliverer to address some of these same cost concerns. The Health Care Financing Administration has adopted a system of rewarding and penalizing physicians based on their performance in the control and reduction of costs (Berenson, 1985). Primary care physicians, who function as 'case managers' in these program, are responsible for providing all primary health care services, as well as coordinating and approving the provision of other health care, including specialty care and hospitalization.

Despite much development and organized system change in many diverse areas of social and health services, there is still mixed evidence that case management efforts have been effective with clients with developmental disabilities (Bertsche & Horejsi, 1980; DeWeaver, 1983; Walker, 1980). With the increasing demand for services for this population and a continuing scarcity of such services, it seems inevitable that the needs of some clients with developmental disabilities will not be fully served (Randolph, et al, 1981) and that the need for development of effective case management will continue. In addition, the evolution of effective case management systems for all clients needing long- term care and coordination of services will continue to be a pressing demand on human services systems for some time to come.

Definitions of Case Management

There is little agreement on the scope and definition of case management, and upon all the activities and functions of persons designated as case managers (National Conference on Social Welfare, 1981). Although definitions of case management differ, there is some growing consensus about the core concepts. Intagliata (1981, p. 102) defines case management as "a process or method for ensuring that consumers are provided with whatever services they need in a coordinated, effective, and efficient manner." He notes that the specific meaning of case management depends on the system that is developed to provide it. For case management systems, two contextual factors are particularly important to consider: (a) the nature of the client population to be served, and (b) the nature of the existing service system. These two factors together shape the goals, functions, and structures that define a given case management system.

Caragonne (1984) proposed that emphasis in case management should focus on service availability, accessibility, responsiveness, continuity, coordination, monitoring/advocacy, and accountability. Case management is appropriate when clients with multiple problems and needs are unable to define, locate, secure, or retain the necessary resources and services of multiple providers on an ongoing basis. The three key components are accountability, accessibility, and coordination. Specifically, Caragonne proposed that the functions of line-service personnel in a case management system are to:

- identify the full range of services needed;
- identify the range of resources available, inclusive of client natural support resources and public community resources;
- coordinate the activities of all services and resources;
- refer clients to all needed resources
- monitor and follow-up to determine if services are received;
- monitor and follow-along to prevent or identify problems in service provision through ongoing contacts with clients, services used, and the clients' natural support resources;
- assess and evaluate the effectiveness of all services/resources utilized.

Several major areas stand out as differentiating the role of the case manager from more traditional social work services roles (Caragonne, 1984). A traditional service model involves office contact between the hours of eight and five, with one service emphasis and little or no interagency contact. A provider has authority relative only to the activities of their case load with little discretionary authority utilized by the case worker. In case management, service settings shift from office-oriented, fixed appointment models to locations where clients live, work, and receive services. Case management focuses on many systems of influence, rather than only on the behaviors of the client. More emphasis is placed on interagency work and relationships. If there are difficulties with other agencies' services or resources, responsibility for resolution rests with the case manager rather than with the client, as it does with more traditional services. In case management, agency accountability rests with all services received by the client, not just those provided by the agency.

Case management involves advocacy, coordination, and monitoring of all collateral resources important to a client's networks of support. Three key areas distinguish traditional models of service from effective case management approaches:

- the scope of intervention in case management includes all relevant client systems;

- line worker autonomy and discretionary authority is commensurate with the added responsibilities and accountability for service delivery; and

- the location of client contact is in a variety of environments and settings.

Despite much theoretical analysis of the differences between case management and traditional social work, Kurtz, Bagarozzi, and Pallane (1984) found that 38% of case management workers in Georgia saw no difference between social work and case management. They suggest that training programs may not be preparing social workers for all aspects of their job requirements.

The conceptual scope of case management has also recently expanded to include much more emphasis on families and on informal networks. For instance, Sister M. Vincentia Joseph and Sister Ann Patrick Conrad (1980) described the use of informal networks in a parish neighborhood model. Seltzer (n.d.) trained family members as case managers for elderly persons in an experimental study supporting the development of partnership between the informal and formal support networks.

Federal Role in Case Management for Persons with Developmental Disabilities

The Developmental Disabilities Act of 1975 (PL 95-602) established case management as a "priority service" and presented it as a mechanism to coordinate service needs in social, medical, educational, and other areas for as long as the services were needed, including lifelong if necessary. The Developmental Disabilities Act defined case management services as:

> ...such services to persons with developmental disabilities as will assist them in gaining access to needed social, medical, educational, and other services; and such terms include—
> (i) follow-along services which ensure, through a continuing relationship, lifelong if necessary, between an agency or provider and a person with a developmental disability and the person's immediate relatives or guardians, that the changing needs of the person and the family are recognized and appropriately met; and
> (ii) coordination services which provide the persons with developmental disabilities support, access to (and coordination of) other services information on programs and services, and monitoring of the person's progress.

Individual plans are required in numerous other federal laws affecting persons with developmental disabilities, including the Rehabilitation Act (PL 93-516) and Education for All Handicapped Children Act (PL 94-142). Case plans are also required or encouraged in Title XX of the Social Security Act (PL 93-647) and Title XIX (Medicaid, PL 94-223). The Developmental Disabilities Assistance Act (PL 95-602) and the Mental Health Systems Act incorporate more specific requirements to establish increased accountability by mandating that every state develop a system of case management to serve the target population.

Research on the Effectiveness of Case Management

Much of the literature on case management is conceptual rather than based upon empirical evaluation studies. For instance, many authors have described issues in case management (e.g., National Council on Social Welfare, 1981) and numerous authors, agencies, and organizations have developed standards for ideal or model case management programs (Morell, Straley, Burris & Covington, 1980; Wray, et al., 1985). Several authors have suggested roles for case management (Ashbaugh, 1981) as a front-line quality assurance and accountability process.

Some case management literature is organizational and efficiency-based, such as work by sociologists, organizational theorists, and industrial psychologists interested in explaining the variations in performance among and within organizations by focusing on worker characteristics, management processes, and organizational structure (Caragonne, 1984). In addition, most research on the empirical effectiveness of case management has been conducted on general social services clients, rather than solely on persons with developmental disabilities. Nevertheless, some of this empirical research is valuable in documenting the advantages of an integrated case management approach and pinpointing difficulties and problems in case management programs.

The majority of the studies of the services integration demonstration projects were site-specific, highly descriptive, and predominantly process-oriented. However, Turner and Washington (Washington, 1974), in an attempt to obtain data on the populations served, developed methods to measure the impact of services provided by the East Cleveland Community Human Service Center. They used measures of client functioning and the behavior of the treated populations as dependent variables. When evaluating the means by which individuals may be moved from levels of dependency toward levels of independence, they concluded that client functioning was enhanced through integrated service systems.

Other evaluations of service integration projects reported that the use of case management teams and case manager linkages led to increases in the accessibility, comprehensiveness, and volume of services provided to clients (Baker & Northman, in press). Caragonne (1979) also reported that the use of case managers led to more effective packaging of client service plans, a greater range of services for clients, documented gaps and duplications in service networks, and generally greater organizational responsiveness to consumer needs.

An integrated rehabilitation service center in Arkansas was evaluated using a research design that compared client outcomes from groups of clients randomly assigned to two traditional and one integrated rehabilitation service program (Roessler & Mack, 1972). Outcome measures were divided into measures of "efficiency" (recidivism, referrals, speed of service, acceptance/referral ratio, agency closures, system closures, and drop outs) and measures of "effectiveness" (client change in attitudes and behavior, reduction of dependency, and client satisfaction). The theory was that more centralized case management and coordination would make services more effective. The conclusion of the study was that such barriers as ineffective leadership, conceptual confusion, and internal agency changes negatively affected the impact of both integrated and more traditional case management programs.

Models in Case Management

Some of the research on case management projects in community support programs has revealed that the use of case managers facilitates client access to services (Maverick Corporation, 1976); provides a necessary administrative link between program and consumer (Rosenberg & Brody, 1974); is more effective in packaging a complex sequence of services than traditional service models (Brody, 1974); documents gaps and duplications in service networks (Perlman, 1975; Bureau of Social Welfare, Maine, 1973); and promotes organization responsiveness to consumer needs (Caragonne, 1979).

One of the most promising models for effective case management is the Direction Service model described by Zeller (1980) and Brewer and Kakalik (1979). Existing programs which have adopted such a model use a client-centered approach and are separate from major service bureaucracies so that focus on a specific service is not emphasized. Determination of who should provide the Direction Service has been debated and the estimated cost per person may diminish its feasibility unless redeployment of existing resources could significantly reduce these costs.

The State of California employs a unique concept in discharging its responsibilities to persons with developmental disabilities. Under the Lanterman Act, 21 regional centers were set up with private non-profit community agencies which were responsible for: (a) identification of persons with developmental disabilities, (b) determination of eligibility of services, (c) purchasing of services, and (d) monitoring and evaluating services according to set standards (May & Hughes, 1987, p. 220). The governing body is drawn from the communities served and one-third of this group must be clients or parents of persons with developmental disabilities. Although centers receive their funding resources from the State, they act as independent brokers of services, purchasing needed services in the market-place. A case manager is assigned who assumes responsibility for the development and implementation of an individual client plan. However, a significant omission in the overall case management system in California was the exclusion of the State hospital system from the Lanterman Act requirements.

Several problems cited by other case management systems are addressed in this model: (a) it provides for direct representation of consumers at all levels of the case management system to ensure accountability and the upholding of consumers' rights; (b) it provides flexibility in the system and addresses the problems of fragmentation and professional separatism; and (c) it shifts the burden of service provision from the bureaucracy to the private sector using an innovative collaboration between public and private enterprise.

Characteristics of Case Managers and Case Management Systems

Some studies have evaluated numerous characteristics of case managers and/or case management systems that might influence the effectiveness of the programs or systems. For instance, Brody (1974) found that caseworkers spend more time in administrative tasks than in providing services to clients. Berkeley Planning Associates (1977) found that system-wide coordination of services, continuity of services to clients, and case manager effectiveness was more likely to occur in small, nonbureaucraticized settings characterized by workers with increased training and education, more years experience in the specific problem field, smaller caseloads, and access to consultation. Also, the quality of case management services appears to be strongly related to the intensity of contact between client and case manager (BPA, 1977).

A number of studies (Baker et al, 1980; Caragonne, 1979; Graham, 1980) have indicated that case managers' activities are significantly shaped by the service systems in which they operate. If, for example, relatively few services are available, case managers spend relatively little time linking clients to services. However, when certain important support services are unavailable, case managers are likely to devote their own time to either directly providing or creating the needed services. Thus, to some degree, case managers' actual activities are ultimately shaped by the constraints of the environments within which they work, rather than by their formal job descriptions.

Evaluations of State Systems

Several states have conducted evaluation studies or surveys of the current status of their case management system. Although these studies will be described in some detail here, it should be taken into account that most recommendations and conclusions generated in these studies were system-specific.

North Dakota conducted a study in 1985 of their case management system (Wray, Basuray, Miller, & Seiler, 1985), which primarily addressed the two different forms of case management in the state: external or regional case management, and internal or service provider case management. The surveyors were charged with making recommendations to reduce duplication between external and internal case management and to recommend a course of action for agencies and providers that would provide an optimum continuum of functions for persons with developmental disabilities. Three groups were surveyed concerning each of the two types of case management: members of the Association for Retarded Citizens, all regional case managers and coordinators, and all service providers.

The surveyors found that despite evidence of a genuine commitment to serving persons with developmental disabilities in policy and funding, and the recognition of the need for a sound case management system, there were indications of problems in communication, and indications that the state's human resources management policies would need to be modified with regard to service providers. Some of the negative factors which were identified as barriers to progress included a feeling of "us-them" between providers, regional and state staff, and consumers and parents. Secondly, specific breakdowns were identified in the training, recruitment, compensation and management of staff in provider organizations. Other problems included lack of leadership in program development by the state. Specific recommendations were made that concerned improving communications between state agencies and providers and parents, reducing paperwork, providing more specific training, resource development of local services to meet individual needs, and clarifying different roles for external and internal case management. The report concluded that there are legitimate service coordination functions to be performed by regional (external) case managers and distinct functions to be performed by program coordinators (internal) in service provider agencies. Extensive recommendations were made regarding the establishment of components of case management, provision of contact points and information and referral, matching clients with case managers, gathering existing data, procuring new assessments, development of individual plans, identification of unavailable services, monitoring services, revision of individual plans, and quarterly reviews by regional case managers.

In the fall of 1982, the case management system in *Kentucky* for persons with developmental disabilities was evaluated by the University Affiliated Facility at the University of Kentucky in response to a request from the state Developmental Disabilities Council and the state office for persons with mental retardation (Human Development Program, 1983). The evaluation method used for fourteen regions in the state was to judge actual performance against a prototype model for case management. The prototype used had been developed by the Rehabilitation Group, Inc. of Virginia. The evaluators proposed that any discrepancies found with the model would suggest that either actual practices or the model itself should be changed or improved.

The evaluation found that the prototype model contained too few administrative standards and too specific delivery standards, and that the roles of the case manager and case manager administrator were inconsistently addressed. Actual practices were not always consistent with the philosophy that should underlie a state-wide case management system. In particular, the issue of advocacy on behalf of the client received varying degrees of attention across the state. When the burden of advocacy was placed on case managers, they had little time to pursue monitoring and evaluation activities. Actual service delivery practices related more closely to the model definition than did administrative practices. Involvement of clients and their families in development of the individual habilitation plan was inconsistent and infrequent.

The evaluation concluded that, despite the many problems, the state was getting a reasonable return for its annual investment. Expenditures for case management were modest and cost effective in relation to total aggregate expenditures for human services. Overall, recommendations were made that case management be provided independently of service-providing agencies, that extensive parent involvement be maintained, and that a variety of agencies be involved in case planning and development. Corrections were recommended to improve policy guidelines; to develop training procedures for case managers, clients, parents, and advocates; and to provide technical assistance from the state level.

South Carolina evaluated its case management system in 1984 by determining whether current practices were in fulfillment of the system's objectives which were set forth at the time the system was put in place in 1979 (Randolph et al., 1984). This state had established a system of free-standing, independent case management agencies, responsible only for the coordination of services under the auspices of the state Developmental Disabilities Council. The evaluation revealed that in large measure the system was meeting its stated objectives and that case coordination had made a difference in enhancing the quality of life for persons with developmental disabilities. Major problems which were identified included public visibility, program operations, administrative relationships, case coordination functions, and interagency relationships. Given the low visibility of programs and the fact that coordinators frequently indicated they were afraid of being flooded with referrals, the case management offices may not have been identifying clients with developmental disabilities who were not being appropriately served. Clients, parents, and providers appeared to have been only perfunctorily involved in development of individual habilitation plans. In addition, it was questionable to what degree the advocacy role of case coordination was being fulfilled.

In 1984, *New York* conducted a time and effort study of their case management system, with one-third of the state's case managers participating in the study (OMRDD, 1984). The major objectives of this study were to identify who received state case management services, what determined the amount of service received, the extent of overlap between state and voluntary case management, and the characteristics of the service systems, such as caseload size and organizational structures. This study found that the three most important variables associated with case management time spent on clients were the case manager's caseload size, the type of client's residence, and whether or not the client belonged to the Willowbrook class of persons deinstitutionalized under court order. Many management and organizational recommendations were made, including ratios of caseload sizes, to facilitate efficiency in the delivery of services.

An evaluation by Caragonne in 1984 of *Georgia's* case management system focused on how actual service activities and procedures compared to the service activities emphasized within the case management model of service. Using an intriguing study design, workers and their administrators at 14 sites were asked to first estimate the percentage of time spent in seven areas of activity: general agency contact, client-specific agency contact, direct services client contact, evaluation activities, recording and reporting, supervision, and travel. When workers estimated the proportion of time spent in each activity, a strong adherence to the case management model was revealed. Supervisors also perceived their workers' activities as congruent with the model, especially in identifying that extensive time was spent in resource development and in arranging services for clients, moderate time in recording/ reporting, and minimal time in supervision and travel. After their initial estimates, workers were asked to record their activities during a ten-day working period. Analysis of actual time and activities revealed a very different picture of time allocation. The data suggested that case managers vastly over-estimated the amount of time they spent in resource development, evaluation, and supervision. Little time was actually spent on the "core" model activities of case management: referral, coordination, follow-up and follow-along, evaluation and advocacy. The study revealed a strong emphasis on in-office work, with over-reliance on problem formulation, planning, and documentation, all strong deterrents to development of effective case management.

The current case management system in Georgia was shown to have three primary features: office-based, administrative in nature, and overly prescriptive and descriptive of client problems. Also, many case managers operated in isolation from their settings, with a striking lack of supervision in the monitoring and support functions of case management. The offices operated in organizational vacuums, isolated within their agency systems, and lacked effective supervision, performance monitoring, and standards by which the quality of work could be judged. One of the six sites was remarkably different than the others in having the highest incidence of activities most in conformance with model case management activities. In an organizational analysis, this site was shown to differ from the others in having the following characteristics: high degrees of perceived leadership; a work climate which emphasized planning and efficiency rather than pressure; high degrees of support from other workers; rules and policies explicitly communicated in a timely, adequate, and effective way; supportive supervision; and moderate degrees of innovation. The site with the least adherence to the case management model of service reported low scores in leadership and task clarity, high degrees of perceived control and pressure, low peer cohesion, little innovation, and little communication.

A *Minnesota* survey of case management personnel in eighty-one county agencies was completed in 1987 to determine the status of case management needs and barriers to effective service delivery to clients with developmental disabilities. Lack of formal training in case management on the part of the majority of directors of county human service agencies, case management supervisors, and case managers was a finding in the Minnesota Case Management Study (McAnally & Linz, 1988). Another major barrier to effectiveness of case management cited was heavy case load size, the majority of case managers averaging over sixty-eight clients with a combined case load of clients both with and without developmental disabilities. Both training and case load size appeared appear to have significant impact on the quality of service provided by the case manager. Recommendations were made to reduce case manager-client ratios and develop relevant training programs.

The case management system in Minnesota was also evaluated in earlier years, both as a separate system and as part of the entire human services system. Two of these studies were conducted by independent consulting firms.

In 1983, an evaluation examining many aspects of the service delivery system for persons with mental retardation was sponsored by the Association of Residences for the Retarded in Minnesota, the Department of Public Welfare, the Minnesota Association of Rehabilitation Facilities, and the Minnesota Developmental Achievement Center Association (Rosenau & Totten, 1983). Regarding case management, five major recommendations were made:

(a) All case managers should have four primary functions: assessing clients' needs, locating and planning services to meet clients' needs, linking and monitoring services, and advocating for the clients and for citizens with mental retardation in general.

(b) Plans should lead toward an ideal of having a case manager client caseload of 1:25.(c) The state should initiate efforts to transfer central funding to case management agencies at the county level.

(d) The state should take the initiative in developing a management information system that addresses the specific human needs of citizens with mental retardation.

(e) Case management should begin with the development of a written plan that specifies ideal client goals and objectives, and specifies a reasonable time framework for moving to the ideal.

The report also recommended that: (a) a clearer statement was needed of the case manager's monitoring responsibilities; (b) the State Department of Human Services should assign major responsibilities for overseeing case management to the counties but should retain limited oversight responsibilities; and (c) case managers should take a productive role in developing a greater number and variety of alternative services and placements.

Also in 1983, under a contract with the Department of Human Services, the Health Planning and Management Resources Inc. (1983) conducted a study of the case management system in Minnesota. They interviewed individuals from state, county, and public and private agencies regarding the current status of case management in their systems, and developed an integrated case management model that could be used by county social services and health agencies in working with disabled adults. This model articulated the role of the case manager. In addition, recommendations were made to the Department of Human Services regarding the development of case management, including training and caseload standards.

The delivery of case management has also been examined by the Court Monitor for the *Welsch v. Levine* consent decree. The semi-annual report (1/84-6/84) of the Monitor noted that case management is a crucial and pivotal component in the delivery of services to persons with developmental disabilities. Problems identified were: (a) conceptualization of the role of case management and managers was restricted; (b) few case managers were qualified or trained for the job; and (c) no commonly available professional training was available for case managers. Recommendations of the report included statewide training, clarification of the case manager role, and monitoring of case management service.

In the following year (1985), the Welsch court monitor conducted a questionnaire survey at the annual conference of the Minnesota Social Services Association. Although responses were primarily from the metropolitan counties, case managers, vendors, institutional staff, county personnel, staff of community programs, psychologists, and special educators were included. The survey identified that in two-thirds of the cases, providers chaired the team meetings for clients. Respondents identified major barriers to effective case management as: (a) caseload size and ratios, (b) lack of adequate services, programs or resources, and (c) training and lack of knowledge. Respondents identified major steps that could be taken to overcome barriers to effective case management in Minnesota in the following order of priority: (a) better qualified case managers and more training and sensitivity; (b) more direction and leadership from the state on the system of service delivery; and (c) better ratios and more client contact. The monitor concluded from the responses that the key issues for persons involved in case management in Minnesota were reduced caseloads, more expertise in developmental disabilities through training, and that the state displayed a lack of leadership, clarity of mission and commitment, as well as bureaucratic confusion and red tape.

Summary

Studies of formal service coordination efforts for persons with developmental disabilities seem to agree that case management systems have the potential for being efficient and effective systems for services coordination. However, regardless of geographic location, several common problems have been identified. Heavy client case loads were commonly cited as a major factor negatively influencing the effectiveness of case managers. Additionally, inadequate training, ineffective leadership, and lack of role clarification were listed as frequent barriers. Characteristics perceived as promoting favorable outcomes were effective leadership, better training programs for case managers, increased involvement of families, supportive supervision, increased client contact, and small case manager-to-client ratios.

References

Ashbaugh, J. (1981). Accountability of community providers for services to the mentally retarded and other developmentally disabled persons: An argument for case manager citizen-based accountability mechanisms. In T.C. Muzzio, J.J. Koshel, & V. Bradley (Eds.), *Alternative community living arrangements and non-vocational social services for developmentally disabled people*. Washington, DC: Urban Institute and Human Services Research Institute.

Baker, F., Intagliata, J., & Kirshstein, R. (1980). *Case Management Evaluation: Second Interim Report*. Tefco Services, Inc. Buffalo, New York.

Baker, F., & Northman, J.E. (in press). *Helping: Human Services for the 80s*. St. Louis: The C.V. Mosby Company, in-press.

Bassuk, E.L., & Gerson, S. (1978). "Deinstitutionalization and Mental Health Services," *Scientific American, 238*, 46-53.

Berenson, R. (July/August, 1985). A physician's perspective on case management. *Business and Health*.

Berkeley Planning Associates (1977). "The quality of case management process: Final Report (Vol. III)," in U.S. Department of Commerce, National Technical Information Service, *The Evaluation of Child Abuse and Neglect Projects 1974-1977*. Washington, DC.

Bertsche, A.V., & Horejsi, C.R. (1980). Coordination of client services. *Social Work, 25*(2), 94-97.

Brewer, G. & Kakalik, J. (1979). *Handicapped children: Strategies for improving services*. New York: McGraw-Hill Book Company.

Brody, R. (1974). *A comparative study of four public social service systems*. Ann Arbor: University of Michigan: Microfilms Limited.

Bureau of Social Welfare, Maine Department of Health and Welfare (1973). *Community needs assessment and study: Social service needs of low-income individuals and families and selected client groups of the Bureau of Social Welfare in Cumberland. York. and Southwestern Counties.* Research, Evaluations, and Planning Unit, Region I: Bureau of Social Welfare, Maine Department of Health and Welfare.

Caragonne, P. (April, 1979). *Implications of case management: A report on research.* Presentation at the Case Management Conference, Buffalo, New York.

Caragonne, P. (1984). Georgia Department of Human Resources, *Developmental Disabilities. Case Management System Evaluation.* Austin, TX: Case Management Research.

DeWeaver, K.L. (1983). Deinstitutionalization of the developmentally disabled. *Social Work, 28(*6), 435-439.

Gans, S., & Horton, G. (1975). *Integration of human services: The state and municipal levels.* New York: Shaeger.

Government Accounting Office. (1976). *Returning the mentally disabled to the community: Government needs to do more.* Comptroller General's Report to the Congress, Washington, DC.

Graham, K. (1980). *The work activities and work-related attitudes of case management personnel in New York State Office of Mental Health Community Support Systems.* Unpublished dissertation, Albany, New York.

Health Planning & Management Resources, Inc. (1983). *Case management: An integrated model.* St. Paul, MN: Department of Human Services, State of Minnesota.

Human Development Program — University Affiliated Facility, University of Kentucky (1983). *Case management to Kentuckians with developmental disabilities: What is it? What should it be?* Executive Summary. Frankfort, Kentucky: Division of Community Services for Mental Retardation, Cabinet for Human Resources.

Intagliata, J. (April, 1981). Operationalizing a case management system: A Multilevel Approach. In *National Conference on Social Welfare: Final Report - Case Management: State of the Art* (Grant No. 54-p-71542/3-01).Submitted to Administration on Developmental Disabilities, U.S. Department of Health and Human Services.

John, D. (1976). *Managing the human services system: What have we learned from services integration?* Washington, D.C.: Project Share.

Joseph, Sr. M. Vincentia & Conrad, Sr. Ann Patrick (September 1980). A parish neighborhood model for social work practice. *Social Casework: The Journal of Contemporary Social Work,* pp. 423-432.

Kakalik, J., Brewer, G., Dougharty, L., Fleischauer, P., & Genensky, S. (1973). *Services for handicapped youth: A program overview.* Santa Monica: The Rand Corporation.

Kurtz, L., Bagarozzi, D., & Pallane, L. (1984). *Case management in mental health: National Association of Social Workers, Inc.*

Lakin, K.C., Bruininks, R.H., Hill, B.K., & Hauber, F.A. (1982). "Turnover of direct care staff in a national sample of residential facilities for mentally retarded people, *American Journal on Mental Deficiency, 87,* 1, 37-42.

Lamb, H.R., & Goertzel, V. (1977). "The long-term patient in the era of community treatment," *Archives of General Psychiatry, 34,* 679-692.

Laski, F., & Spitalnik, D. (1979). A review of Pennhurst implementation. Community Services Forum, 1(1), 1, 6, and 8.

Litvin, M.E., & Browning, P.L. (1978). Public assistance in historical perspective. In J. Wortis (Ed.), *Mental retardation and developmental disabilities: An annual review.* New York: Brunner/Mazel.

Maverick Corporation. (1972-75). *The community life association.*

May, D., & Hughes, D. (1987). Organizing services for people with mental handicap: the California experience. *Disability. Handicap. and Society, 2*(3), 213-230.

Mittenthal, S. (1975). *Human service development projects in sixteen allied service (SITO) projects.* Wellsley, MA: The Human Ecology Institute.

Morell, J.E., Straley, C.I., Burris, C.I., & Covington, E. (1980). *Design specifications for case management / service coordination and individualized planning.* Falls Church, VA: Rehab Group, Inc.

National Conference on Social Welfare. (April, 1981). *Final report - Case management: State of the art.* Grant No. 54-P-7 1542/3-01. Submitted to Administration on Developmental Disabilities, United States Department of Health and Human Services.

Office of Management and Budget. (1978). *Information and referral for people needing human services - a complex system that should be improved*. Report to Congress by the Comptroller General of the United States, General Accounting Office, Washington, DC.

Office of Mental Retardation/Developmental Disabilities. (1984). *Case management time and effort study: Final report*. Albany, NY: OMRDD, State of New York.

Office of the Monitor for the *Welsch* Decree. (April, 1985). Results of case management questionnaire. St. Paul, Minnesota.

Perlman, R. (1975). *Consumers and social services*. New York: John Wiley and Sons.

President's Panel on Mental Retardation. (1962). *A proposed program for national action to combat mental retardation*. Washington, DC: U.S. Government Printing Office.

Randolph, J.L., Spurrier, P.G., & Abramczyk, L. (1984). An evaluation of the South Carolina Developmental Disabilities Case Coordination System. Columbia, SC: South Carolina Developmental Disabilities Council.

Rice, R. (April, 1977). A cautionary view of allied services delivery. *Social Case Work*.

Richardson, E. (1971). Interdepartmental memorandum: Services integration in HEW: An initial report. Washington, D.C., Department of Health, Education, and Welfare.

Roessler, R.T., & Mack, G. (Winter 1972). Services integration: Here to stay? *Research and Practice Review, 4*, 35-43.

Rosenau, N., & Totten, C. Case management services in Minnesota. St. Paul, MN: Association of Residences for the Retarded in Minnesota.

Rosenberg, M., & Brody, R. (1974). *Systems serving people*. Cleveland: Case Western Reserve.

Segal, S., & Aviram, V. (1978). *The mentally ill in community-based sheltered care*. New York: John Wiley & Sons.

Seidl, F., Applebaum, R., Austin, C., & Mahoney, K. (1983). *Delivering in-home services to the abed and disabled: The Wisconsin experiment*. Lexington, MA: Lexington Books.

Seltzer, M.M. (undated). *Family members as case managers: Partnership between the formal and information support networks.* Boston, MA: Boston University School of Social Work.

Simpson, D.F. (1982). *Case management in long-term care programs.* Washington, D.C.: Center for the Study of Social Policy.

Walker, P.W. (1980). Recognizing the mental health needs of developmentally disabled people. *Social Work, 25*(4), 293-297.

Washington, R.O. (1974). *Second year evaluation report of the East Cleveland Community Human Service Center.* Cleveland: School of Applied Social Sciences.

Weil, M., Karls, J.M., et al (1985). *Case Management in Human Service Practice: A Systematic Approach to Mobilizing Resources for Clients.* San Francisco: Jossey-Bass Publishers.

Willer, B., Scheerenberger, R.C., & Intagliata, J. (1978). Deinstitutionalization and mentally retarded persons, *Community Mental Health Review, 3,* 1-12.

Wray, L.D., Basuray, M.T., Miller, H., & Seiler, D.V. (1985). *Working together to meet the needs of North Dakotans with developmental disabilities: Regional developmental disabilities and service provider roles in service coordination.* Falcon Heights, Minnesota.

Wray, L. & Wieck, C. (1985). Moving persons with developmental disabilities toward less restrictive environments through case management. In K. Charlie Lakin & Robert H. Bruininks, (Eds.), *Strategies for Achieving Community Integration of Developmentally Disabled Citizens.* Baltimore, MD: Paul H. Brookes Publishers, pp. 219.

Zeller, R. W. (1980). Direction service, collaboration one case at a time, J.O. Elder, & P.R. Magrab, (Eds.), *Coordinating Services to Handicapped Children.* Baltimore, MD: Paul H. Brookes Publishers.

CHAPTER II

Organizing the Community

by John McKnight

T here is a big problem in my talking about community because everybody is an expert. Every one of you is a member of a community and has direct experience and knowledge.

I have a big problem because you know about the community. The only way I think I can add anything to what you already know is perhaps to give you some new words or new ways of addressing what is your own experience.

If, as I speak about community, it doesn't seem that way to you, then I must be wrong because I am really talking *with* you about what you know from your experience, though perhaps in a slightly different language.

My neighbor, Mary, has a young daughter, Cynthia, about four years old. Mary, who lives about four houses away, called me and said she wanted to come over and talk to me. I wondered what the trouble was—was I not cutting the lawn often enough, or what was wrong? When she arrived, she was obviously concerned and upset about something. I realized she wanted to talk to me because I was the only person on the block who was from a university. She had a problem about education so she picked me out as her counselor, not knowing that I didn't know anything at all about her concerns. She thought a professor must know.

She said, "John, I have got to talk with you because something is troubling me about Cynthia."

I asked, "What is it?" Cynthia seemed to me a wonderfully normal young girl.

She said, "Cynthia is four years and three months old. The problem is that she can read."

I said, "Well, what is the problem?"

She said, "All the other mothers on the block who have children older than we do say that at Nichols School, the teachers don't like to have children coming to the school who know how to read, because they usually do not know how to read right. They have to break them of the way they've learned how to read in order to teach them the right way. I am afraid that we have hurt Cynthia's life chances by her reading."

She added, "Mind you, we did not teach her." She wanted to assure me that she would not have done such a terrible thing to her daughter as teach her to read at four years of age.

I was stunned by that conversation. I checked with the principal at Nichols School, and Mary was right. They do not like to have children come there who know how to read because at the school they teach them to read in a developmental way, in the proper order and sequence with the proper methods. So I realized that, indeed, Cynthia's mother was being taught by professionals *not* to educate her daughter.

The day after my conversation with Mary, I was talking to my next door neighbor, Frank, and I told him the story about Cynthia. Frank said, "Oh yeah, I know about that. You know John Pisak, who lives down the block, is chief coach of the Little League. He is concerned because there are a lot of young kids who go over to Nichols school yard with a bat and ball and play baseball. They are all learning how to play the wrong way and they are not being properly prepared, in terms of their own safety—now, don't laugh. After all, it is unsafe for those kids to be there playing baseball on their own. And he is going to try to do something through the Little League in the way of parent education—*parent education*—that will ensure that parents do not allow kids to play baseball unsupervised outside of Little League jurisdiction."

The next week, I went to my parents' home for my mother's 75th birthday. I was sitting around, talking with my mother and I told her about Cynthia, and about the Little League.

She said, "Oh, I see that every place."

Then she went on to tell me about how things were when she was young.

She said, "You know, almost everybody I knew learned to read at home. When I was a kid, everybody in the neighborhood watched after kids. When we had a family problem, everybody in the family got together and talked about the family problem. If we had a fight between two people in the neighborhood, everybody knew there was a fair person you could turn to. The sidewalks were covered with white marks from stones that kids found for hopscotch. At parties, people played charades. Children were mostly taken care of by children. It was at dinner that you told stories and discussed the issues of the day. We actually lived in a house that my father and brother built."

I thought about her story and realized that things really had changed in the 75 years of her life because education has left the community and gone into the school and become the jurisdiction of the teacher. The responsibility for young people's behavior left the community and became the domain of the criminal justice system and youth workers. Family problems became the jurisdiction of social workers; disputes, the jurisdiction of lawyers; health, the jurisdiction of doctors. Hopscotch and charades have been replaced by recreational directors and television. Child care has become a profession; dinner is the jurisdiction of McDonalds. The news of the day is the jurisdiction of ABC, NBC and CBS. And houses come from Century 21.

There are a lot of people in the United States who will say to you that families are falling apart here. Look at the divorce rate. They would have you believe that the reason is that something has happened between men, women and children that makes them unable to live together effectively.

After listening to my mother, I understood the reason families are having a lot of trouble is because they don't have anything to do. At one time families existed to perform functions and solve problems, but now we may not need families. If education is handled by the school, behavior is handled by the police, family relations by social workers, disputes by lawyers, health by doctors, play by recreational directors, children's lives handled by child care workers, their meals by Colonel Sanders, the understanding of the day's events by Mr. Rather, and houses by Century 21, then I think it's apparent that families will not fare well—because they have nothing to do.

So, there is a real trade-off, as we see more and more of our lives becoming professionalized and commercialized. One result is that individuals have diminished initiatives and competencies. Families are also diminished and weakened as systems grow. As schools grow stronger, as criminal justice systems grow, as social work systems grow, as legal systems grow, as medical systems grow, as recreational systems grow, as child care systems grow, *families diminish* in responsibility and competence.

The human group is not something that is inevitable; we have come together in human groups for the purpose of doing things, solving problems and enjoying each other. If these functions of the human group are taken away, the group will dissolve. As professional systems have laid claim over more and more of your life and mine, the result is that individual and group incompetence has grown.

A woman who got a Ph.D. in our department came into my office on her graduation day to say good-bye and sat down and cried. I felt bad that she and the other people who had worked on a challenging project were going, and I thought she was crying because she was leaving. But she wasn't. She said, "I realize that I am finally here. I have my Ph.D. and I know now what I have. I know more about less than anybody in the world. I have learned infinitely about a tiny, tiny piece of the world. But I cannot sew a dress; I cannot build a house. I may not be very good at social relations either."

I think we are all seeing the same thing in our communities. They are not working very well. And I think, like the Ph.D. student, we see the same thing in individuals—they do not know how to do very much. Primarily, but not exclusively, the reason for this is the growth and power of our professions, our systems, and the technology they use. Or, to put it another way, as schools grow more powerful and influence the minds and behavior of more parents on my block, the education in my community will decrease. Each of these systems has taken power, money, authority, and legitimacy from individuals, families, and communities. The real dilemma of our time is how to reverse that process. That is why I am addressing issues of community.

Systems and communities are in competition for the lives of people. As systems grow bigger and more powerful, with more authority, money and legitimacy, families, communities, and the human group diminish in power, competence, potence, authority, and capacity. The result is a world where systems have overwhelmed and finally decimated communities and families. This leads to the creation of some strange new forms of life like the "health consumer."

Now my mother believes that health has to do with how you live your life. When I was a child, she made certain, in her ignorance, that I had on my plate every day a green vegetable, some protein and some starch and a little plate of fruit. My poor mother thought that was really the origin of good health. She was anxious that I get out and play baseball with the other people because she thought that kids exercising was an important part of their development and their health. My confused mother believes, even to this day, that if I would get out every day and start walking around, and stop eating all the desserts that I eat, I would not be as heavy as I am and I would be healthier. She even believes that she can go out in her back yard and pick the leaves of some plants and make tea out of them and cure most of the problems that I have—my poor confused mother believes that. But that's because my poor confused mother was raised in a community where they believed that health was a condition created by effective families and good communities.

But now, most of us are raised in a world of systems where we know that health comes from a health system. When that system works, it produces health, and we are "health consumers."

When my mother was young there were no health consumers because you could not consume health; there was no system that was supposed to produce health. There were only doctors who treated illness. My mother was just a human being who had to join her family, neighbors and community in doing the things that would make them healthy. But I can now sit and not walk around, and eat all the sweets I want because the University of Minnesota has a big medical center that produces health. Professionals will do that for me; I need not worry, as my mother did, about all that health stuff. And I need not teach my kids what she taught me, because health is now a system.

As a health consumer, I am the individual raw material for a system and the University of Minnesota's Medical Center needs me. And I need them because I do not have a community.

So there is a competition between systems and communities for how problems get solved, how we know things and how we enjoy life. Every health care professional is a part of that competition, not just in a professional sense but in their very lives because they are also citizens and members of a community. One of the ways this competition shows up in my life is that when I see a problem that neither I, nor my neighbors, nor my family believe we are capable of solving, we say that we need professional help. More and more, when there is a problem, I hear somebody say, "She needs professional help; he needs professional help." What they are saying is that families and communities are incompetent but professionals are competent and know better.

Let me explain what I mean by the word community. I think communities are made up of groups of people who come together to enjoy each other and to solve problems on a face-to-face basis. Groups of people who control their group and who are not agents of systems.

A community is made up of people, families, neighbors and neighborhood organizations, clubs, civic groups, self-help groups, ethnic associations, temples, churches, local businesses, sports groups, veterans organizations, local media, local government, local unions. The community is a set of associations which, working together, represent how people who have taken authority for their lives come together to create the tools to solve life's problems. That authority and responsibility is constantly threatened by the growth of professional systems.

My wife once said to me, "You are always talking about systems versus communities. Let me give you some better names. Systems are the empire— as in *The Empire Strikes Back*. Communities are the homeland. You're actualy describing the struggle between the empire and the homeland."

The struggle between the empire and the homeland goes on in your life every day. It's a struggle over families, over the lives of children, over the lives of the elderly, and over the lives of people called "disabled."

When I was a child in a little town in Ohio, both among the children and the adults in my daily life, there were people who were what you would call "labeled people." Wherever I went in my town, I was likely to see people with some kind of disability. When I was a child, those people lived in the homeland. As I grew up, those people disappeared. Something reached into the community and took them away—literally. You can go to my little home town today and walk around and not see any of the labeled people who used to be present as part of our everyday life. The empire took them away. We had a homeland from which we exiled hundreds of our people. Your current role is to get them back. This terrible struggle in which systems have overwhelmed and hurt communities is what gives you your jobs. Because your job is to try to correct that terrible, evil thing that happened.

This is a struggle over whether people are going to be citizens or whether they are going to be clients. The empire is the land of clients; the community is where the citizens live. It is a struggle between living in a world of service or in a community where there is some care. System service is second-rate community care.

There's a wonderful schlock furniture store two blocks from my home which always has big signs in the window saying they are selling a complete dining room and living room set for $76.00.
The other day there was a rocker recliner in the window for only $79.00; in the corner of the sign were the words, "Genuine Vinyl!" It made me think that service is to care as genuine vinyl is to wool.

There is a struggle between service and care; also a struggle over whether we are going to live in a world of control or consent. Systems are the way you organize things if you want to have very few people controlling a lot of people. That is why the system is diagrammed as a set of boxes with one box at the top and lots of boxes at the bottom—a very accurate representation of the empire.

There are thousands of ways of getting people together to solve problems. Our hierarchical system is only one way of many; it is the one you use when you want a few people controlling the lives of many people. It is great for fighting wars, running ships, and making automobiles, but it probably does not help human beings in their relationships or capacities. If you want to help human beings with their relationships, capacities, care and citizenship, you have to get them out of the system. Ultimately, systems are anti-democratic; they are about a few controlling many. If I want to live in a country where few control many, I know where to go. I choose to stay here because that is what I do not want. I want America to be the homeland of citizens, of care, of consent.

The struggle between the empire and the homeland goes on every day. It goes on in your personal lives and you are a part of that struggle. You are also in the middle of the struggle between systems and communities for the lives of labeled people. One can do case management and be a social worker whose work will systematically hurt and injure community; such people are, perhaps unknowingly, the agents of the empire, diminishing the authority and capacity of community. If you are that kind of case manager or case worker, you need to be retrained. There are all kinds of professional people who are agents of the empire, and whose unintended function is, in truth, hurting community. The other possibility is that you are at heart a member of the homeland and your work strengthens community capacity because it is mainly about connecting people to the resources and capacities of their communities for problem solving.

Let me share with you some ideas that may help you decide whether you are an agent of the empire or a part of the homeland. The empire has become tremendously strong, but at the same time one can see all kinds of examples of a regenerating force coming forward from the community. Anyone concerned about the well-being of labeled people needs to have as their main purpose the regeneration of community and the capacity of communities to accept the contributions of people who have labels.

What is regenerating community? Let me give you one or two examples. A new profession developed in the 1920s. This profession began taking responsibility for women's bodies. Women's bodies, from the birth of humankind until the 1920s, were the property of women and of women in community. But this profession in the twenties began to say, "No, women's bodies are our responsibility"
—just like the school saying Cynthia's learning to read was their responsibility.

The professionals were called pediatricians and ob-gyn *men*. They were men laying claim on women's bodies. The profession became very powerful, their empire grew. By the time I was born, they were so powerful and strong that they had convinced most women that one of the worst things they could do was breast feed. Women would have been embarrassed to say they had breast fed. The profession made many women think it was a harmful and bad thing. They swept across the community; they overwhelmed the minds of women. The majority of women in the United States came to believe that it was not a good idea to breast feed.

In 1948, in a suburb of Chicago called Oak Park, there was a young mother who tried to breast feed; she was eccentric. She could not get the milk to flow so she called her ob-gyn man and he told her why that was a bad idea. She called her pediatrician and he told her why it was a bad idea. She was bull-headed, going against all the professional advice of the empire. She hunted around until she found an older woman who still remembered how to make the milk flow and this woman helped her. Then a neighbor of the young woman saw her breast feeding and came over and talked to her about it. The neighbor decided to breast feed her newly arrived baby. Because they were both doing this against the wisdom of the pediatric and ob-gyn empire, they gave each other mutual support by getting together and sharing their feelings about breast feeding. Other women in Oak Park heard about them and said, "Could we join you? Though we're told we should not breast feed, we do not agree." So they formed a mutual support club. Other women heard the women in the community saying, "The empire's wrong! Professionals do not know! We should re-claim our bodies!"

It spread like wildfire, not only across the United States but around the world. There are now thousands of these clubs around the world. They are called the Leche League; "leche" is Spanish for "the milk." Around the world, women are getting together, sharing and affirming the power of the community and of women over their bodies. So we know it is possible for people working together at the community level to resist the empire and take its authority and privilege away and bring it back Home.

Another example is happening in your field where there are people who are regenerating community by stealing people with disabilities from the empire and bringing them back to the homeland. I have asked people who are engaged in this activity to write me about their experiences. Recently I received a letter from a woman in Louisville, Kentucky, who would be called a "social service professional" by the person who hired her. However, she is like the women in the Leche League. She has made her job into support for the community by stealing people from the system and bringing them into community life. She wrote me about a teenager named Tyrone who is not given to speaking, so he says nothing. She found Tyrone in a group home. Group homes are small versions of the empire. She tried to ascertain Tyrone's capacity because most people thought Tyrone couldn't do anything. After watching Tyrone, she decided that he had a wonderful ability to relate to animals. She looked around Tyrone's community, in his homeland, and found a little pet store called Pets Galore.

The woman wrote me as follows:

"I went to Pets Galore to see how Tyrone was doing. Tyrone goes to the pet store to help feed the animals each afternoon. He goes there three afternoons alone and two afternoons with one of our workers. Tyrone loves to go and my assistant had reported that everything was going well. When I arrived, Verna, the woman who owns the store, escorted me to her office. When we walked in, there was a huge cat lying on the floor. Verna turned around and yelled `Tim, Tyrone let the cat out again!'

"I immediately began feeling very anxious about Tyrone and his behavior. She began the conversation by saying that they were having some problems with Tyrone. She said that Tyrone tries to water the rats and he cannot get the tube in the water bottle correctly so it sometimes pops off and drowns all the baby rats. Also, they have a Coke dispenser and candy bars for their staff and it operates on an honor system; you leave money in the box. They discovered Tyrone was drinking four to five Cokes a day and helping himself to the candy and not putting any money in the box. Well, I was listening to all of this as a human service worker. I was trying to figure out how to fix it because I thought she was just about to tell me that Tyrone could not come any more.

"I told Verna that we could take care of things and Mimi, my assistant, could train Tyrone to do what she wanted him to do, and we would make sure he did not take any more Cokes.

"Verna said they had already taken care of the Coke situation because they closed and locked the door when Tyrone came in. That made sense to me. She went on to tell me how proud Tyrone acted when he rode in the truck with her other workers and how he responded better to men than to her and Mimi. She said he cuts up with the men. A few times customers have asked him questions and he either points or leads them to the desk for the appropriate thing. They have learned to understand his gestures and when he goes to the steps and makes a sound he is asking if he should go downstairs.

"She told me a story about a man who had known Tyrone in school. He came into the store and commented to Verna that he could not believe how polite and friendly Tyrone acted now. He asked how Verna had done it.

"Verna said that she thought they could do better with Tyrone than we could with our staff because our staff wanted him to be perfect and wanted him to do more than he was capable of doing. She said that Tyrone gets obstinate when you push him. Listening to this woman, I realized that we viewed Tyrone from different perspectives. Verna sees Tyrone for what he is; he is not perfect by any means. In fact, he makes lots of mistakes, but the people at the pet store adapt to him. They see Tyrone as an individual and as important; it is obvious that they care about him.

"I realized that Mimi and I had looked at Tyrone's inadequacies as problems needing to be fixed. This, of course, is the classic example of the professional role. I told Verna that she was absolutely right and I tried to explain about the human service mentality. I told her that we need to listen more to citizens like her. Verna went on to say that all handicapped people needed was to be involved, like Tyrone. Involved in community, like Tyrone. Verna was proud that she was a part of something that was good for people."

Every time something like this happens, I learn from it. I am learning to trust citizens more. I feel more hope now for the future. I see how easy it is to act as citizens rather than as professionals. Tyrone goes to Pets Galore five afternoons a week now. Every day he goes alone. So he is home. He no longer has a social service professional helping him. Tyrone does not need the empire any more.

It is good to remind oneself of what composes the community. All these associations and groups controlled by people rather than managers. You have to bring a Tyrone to someone like Verna in order for Tyrone to have a place. You cannot bring him to a *system*. We have no room for Tyrone at Northwestern University because we are a system. Verna was able to find room.

I lived half my life in a little town in Wisconsin called Spring Green. I talked to four people in Spring Green and asked them to tell me about all the groups there. This is a town of 1,700 people, 800 of them adults, most of them married—400 families. The four people I talked to gave me the names of the groups they knew of. This added up to 88 groups. If 400 families create this many groups (actually, there are more than 100), then people with disabilities who live in Spring Green are in a context rich with the associations of community.

When people tell me, "I'm a community worker; my job is to get people involved in community. I am concerned about the community and people with disabilities or labeled people," I think immediately that this is where they are—in the community. They know the leaders of these kinds of local groups and are themselves involved in these kinds of associations. This is what I think they are talking about.

But often I find that what they really mean when they say they are involved in community work is that they attend agency meetings, which consist of people from the empire meeting together and talking *about* community. This is *not* community.

If I were to measure any agency dealing with people with disabilities that was dedicated to getting them home again, I would ask every single worker, "How many people with disabilities have you been around, in touch with this week?" If the answer is "none," then my answer is, "You ain't serious. You are kidding yourself, your clients, and/or the community—because *this* is where the community is."

CHAPTER III

Content and Politics of Case Management

by Allan Bergman

A phenomenal amount of change is occurring in our society, and particularly in service delivery to people with the label "developmentally disabled."

Richard Ferris, former Chairman of the Board of United Airlines made a statement that is as pertinent to the area of service delivery as it is to aviation. He said, "The one constant in society today is change." Most people in their professional education, be it social work, psychology, special education, rehabilitation, or outside of human services, did not receive course work on how to cope with this constant state of flux. Consequently, what often happens is that people become institutionalized in their ways of doing problem solving and delivering services. How fortunate it would be if there were a magic formula today on how to be prepared for rapid change, but perhaps the best solution available is to accept the fact that most of what was learned in formal education and in training experiences is likely to be irrelevant to the task at hand.

Why did you pay so much for tuition? Or why are you still paying off your student loan? It is because so many job descriptions stipulate that you have to have certain initials after your name in order to do the work. Increasingly, that premise is being challenged around the country and is being replaced by a statement of competencies that people need to have to accomplish a mission, once that mission has been identified. This shift is a much needed change in the business of human services.

The formal beginning of service systems for people with so called "developmental disabilities" began in the late '40's and early '50's and precipitated a whole new beginning in how we think about <u>community</u>. This community system was actually begun by those parents who did not want to place their family members in a state facility called a public institution.

We have come a long way in 35 years and perhaps we should reflect on how fast we are changing. In 1976, a major federal legislative entitlement called SSI was passed. That was never in the vision of the early pioneers, advocates, parents and professionals. SSI stipulates that you are entitled to a cash grant in this country just for being here and being "severely disabled."

We got it! And along with it, access to Title 19, Title 20, food stamps and a whole series of "empire-latent services." Now, several years later, we have gone from a 26-year gap to a ten-year gap. This started in 1980 when a new thrust centered around employment, preferably integrated supported employment— which seems to indicate that SSI had been a disincentive. It was holding people back from the new values, the new change. Hopefully, by the time this Congress concludes its business, a major piece of legislation will have passed which will not allow SSI to continue as a disincentive to people in their becoming employed and earning wages.

The resistance to this change by the federal empire has been *phenomenal*. The resistance has not been as great in the field, although there has been some. The real resistance, however, has been in the Social Security Administration. It had a whole series of forms, policies, and procedures in place to administer a cash grant assistance program, as well as access to Medicaid and other services. The perceived reality was that all the people receiving those checks were unemployable. Then, a group of "up-starts" came along, usually in university settings, showing a correlation between a score on an IQ test and an individual's ability to be economically productive. We showed them people with disabilities *working*, and the establishment believed that those were the exceptions. They thought that something had to be wrong. Obviously there was an inaccurate diagnostic work-up. Such was the attitude of the Social Security Administration in the early 1980s.

Now, they have finally "bought into" the new concept. Legislation passed which will no longer take away Medicaid, medical assistance and health insurance, if, in fact, the person with disabilities becomes employed and no longer meets the financial eligibility criteria for SSI. We have convinced people in enough places around the country that, in fact, severe disability is not synonymous with dependence or unemployability or day training, day activity, work activity or sheltered workshops. This is part of the change that is occurring; a fascinating change and a fascinating opportunity.

People in human services should do some reading outside the field and devote a little time to the bigger world. A larger perspective is important in the field of human services and in the area of developmental disabilities. We are only a small part of society. It is helpful to know what else is going on and what other people are thinking. Publications such as *Future Shock* or *Third Wave* give us a better sense of what else is happening in the world where we all live and how we, in our preferred vision of the future, need to be serving people with developmental disabilities so they can live, learn, work and play in their respective communities.

Rapid, rapid change is occurring and it is exciting!

For example, the term "case management," like the term "client," WAS a good term. Certainly the principles intended were good. That term really came about as a result of the Panel for Mental Retardation in 1962—a long time ago. In 1974, it was incorporated into the Developmental Disabilities Act, and it has also been a priority issue under federal legislation. We should stop and think about the implications of the term,"case management." How many people do you know to whom we have attributed a label really want to be known as a *case*, and how many really want to have their lives *managed*?

Language is a very powerful tool. What does that term communicate to those outside of our system? If we say to a citizen that we are "case managers," what might their perception of that be? We need to call it what it is, or what it should be, and that is "service coordination." If you go back to the President's Panel of 1962, the reason given for needing case managers was that we were beginning to develop a variety of service agencies, mechanisms, and public funding strains for people labeled as developmentally disabled, and there needed to be coordinators and someone to help folks access these services. As we continue to clarify our values, it is becoming clear that this task requires a facilitator and an enabler—a negotiator. Most of us did not get a lot of professional training in how to do those things.

The discipline of social work has come a long way from the original concepts of the case work and community work of Jane Addams. She knew what service coordination and community integration were all about. But as I understand it from my friends who are professional social workers, there are only three programs in the country today at the university level that teach community organizing, community integration, and community access as major disciplines in the school of social work.

Another problem present in many disciplines is that until very recently there has been a lack of discussion about accountability and outcome, particularly in the field of human services. This is a luxury that we can no longer afford. The bill payers and people who receive services are beginning to say, "It doesn't make a difference." Didn't it make a difference that we spent X million dollars last year? This is big business. At the federal, state, and county levels we are now spending around 20 to 25 billion dollars a year—taxpayer money—on developmental disabilities. It may not be enough. One reason why there is a lot of waste and inefficiency might be because we are still struggling with *why* we do it. The answer is in the Developmental Disabilities Act where we have declared the values. They are simple in some ways—independence, productivity, and integration. This is no longer philosophical rhetoric mouthed by rebel advocates. This is the law of the land. All services to persons with developmental disabilities must result in increased independence, increased productivity, and integration into the community. That is the law.

Service coordinators become a critical element in helping people achieve those outcomes. But what has happened in the names of technology, and of goals and objectives, is that we have tended to focus on independence and productivity. We have done very little in really getting into the community— a real community. In most states, the "community-based" delivery system is, in fact, just that. A base—it is *not* the community. We have set up a system which is often isolated, segregated, and only minimally connected with the rest of the community.

Life is a series of contracts, choices, and connections. A woman named Beth Mount developed something called "the community contact map." To develop this map, you are asked to think about and plot your life experiences and people contacts over the course of a seven day week. Take that same map and think about somebody you know who is in "the system", who has a label, and either ask them or plot out to the best of your knowledge, the contacts they have. Most of us, when we finish that map, have listed anywhere from 100 to 500 people contacts with assorted kinds of lifestyles. Most people in the system have no more than 8 to 15 contacts, or if they have done exceptionally well, they could have 25. And, almost exclusively, those contacts are other people with labels and people we called "paid staff." That is not community. That is not *real* community.

The challenge of the next decade is not to stop doing what we are doing in terms of competencies and functional skill acquisition, but the challenge is to get serious about how to do it better. Do we really know how to get into the neighborhood association? If improvements do not occur, it is question-able whether people are significantly better off and whether we have really achieved what this business is all about. People need friends, and people need connections.

A good example is an agency from Colorado. Administratively, they decided to get out of the group home business. They realized that eight people living together with staff was not the preferred way for people to live. They are now primarily using apartments, some small duplex housing, but in most cases, people are either living with one or two other people with support staff who may be there 24 hours a day, or as little as an hour a day, depending on the real support needs of that individual. It is not a facility-based model. What is even nicer is that part of the responsibility of the staff is to help make connections in the neighborhood where these people live.

There is a particular gentleman named Sam who lived in the institution. His father is elderly, and several years ago he was one of those people who was de-institutionalized to the group home. His father was worried about it (his mother was deceased), but he said, "Okay, we'll give it a try." A couple of years later the same agency came along and said "We think it will now be better for Sam to live in an apartment." Sam's father was not thrilled about that, but having some trust in the staff, he said, "Let's try." After six months of living in his new situation, Sam was beginning to have some problems. A staffing was called, but this was not the usual kind of staffing with a group of paid staff. Generally, it is those who have an investment in this person who come to the table to do the problem-solving. In this case, many other people had become invested in Sam—people in the community who had developed relationships with him. Twenty of those people came to the staffing. Only seven of the people at the table were paid staff. They did some non-traditional, human service problem-solving because different people in the neighborhood made suggestions and agreed to assume responsibility for certain activities and certain functions. When it was all over, Sam's father went to the director and said, "I guess everything is going to be okay for Sam. I don't need to worry any more." That's powerful. In terms of the security and stability issues with which parents deal, Sam's father has seen that his son has a support system of friends and neighbors who are not paid to be invested in his life, but have CHOSEN to be his support system.

This wonderful example does not mean there is no role for paid professionals. There is plenty of work to be done, but roles, missions, and tasks are rapidly changing. If it is clear that the purpose of servicing is to be a servant, using McKnight's paradigm, we must answer the question, "Whom do we serve?—the empire, or the individual with the label?" All of us, but particularly case managers, service coordinators, and social workers, must direct loyalties and responsibilities to the person receiving services. Clearly in order to do this, case managers or service coordinators cannot work for the entity that runs the program. There is an inherent conflict of interest. "The boss" has to keep the six beds in the group home full, or the fifty spaces in the sheltered workshop full, and that is what facility managers have to do. It can be a real tug-of-war trying to determine whom you are really there to serve: the budgets and needs of the agency, or the people? The people. If you are clear on that, the rest comes easily.

To emphasize why we need to become serious about integrations, about friendships, about relationships, let us look at some of the data from a Lou Harris poll conducted in 1985, examining practices relating to people with disabilities. These data clearly indicate that progress has been made in terms of independence, productivity, and community integration for people with disabilities during the last twenty to thirty years. However, here are some of the other conclusions:

> Disabled Americans participate much less often in a host of social activities than other Americans regularly enjoy, including watching movies, plays, sports events, and going to restaurants. Nearly two-thirds of all Americans with disabilities did not go to a movie in the past year. (Harris, 1986)

Some of us did not go to a movie last year, but we did it as a conscious choice. It is probable that most of the people with disabilities were never provided with the opportunity to go to a movie. That is very different. People with disabilities are three times more likely than non-disabled people never to eat in restaurants. Three-fourths of people with disabilities did not see live theatre or a live music performance in the past year; for the non-disabled population, it was only one-third. These are statistically significant differences.

Disability also has a negative impact on vital daily activities like shopping for goods. A much higher proportion of persons with disabilities, than without disabilities, never shop in a grocery store. How many of us buy food from the institutional bulk food delivery systems? Creating procedures which reduce opportunities for community experiences are often viewed as necessary for the logistical organization of group living. However, the people who live in group situations are there to acquire training for independence—and yet they may never get the opportunity to go to the grocery store with a real shopping list. This is sometimes the consequence when logistical organization supercedes critical goals. This may be done with the best of intentions, but remember that we are in a time of accelerating change which presents some of the most exciting opportunities to accomplish the preferred vision of the future. Those of you who have chosen to be the coordinators, the facilitators, the enablers, will be pivotal in seeing that, to the greatest extent possible, we increase the opportunities for people to choose and to have control over their own environment through empowerment activities. Empowerment does not imply total independence. None of us are totally independent. We are all inter-dependent. This term suggests the ability to exert greater control over one's own life. That is what independence is about—decision-making, choices, reduced dependency on someone else to determine what is best for you and to do things for you. Sometimes, the helping professions paradigm creates within us a need to be needed. We have to rethink that and make sure that it is not a barrier in letting somebody go, or in giving people the opportunity to grow, develop, and make mistakes. Mistakes are all a part of normal growth and development. It does not mean doing something insane like taking someone labeled profoundly, multiply impaired and telling them to take the bus as a way of getting independent, saying "Good luck!". That's perverse. But it does mean giving people the opportunity in a REAL setting to make mistakes and to develop problem-solving skills that result from those mistakes.

We must think through the process to the desired end product. What is the outcome? Why are we spending 25 billion dollars on this population in this country? I think we know now. As we change models, we must consciously avoid getting locked into one model. With changes occurring as rapidly as they are today, we can be sure that today's Utopian model is tomorrow's Model T. That is how fast we are learning new approaches.

We must be clear on our mission and on our values to avoid disruption as service models change. Relinquishing more and more power to the person we are being paid to serve is a reason for celebration. Many of the services which were previously being paid for are now being done by the individual or by the community, friends, neighbors, and co-workers. This becomes the challenge to the system—the challenge of strategic planning. This must become the goal of service coordination. If we are clear on that, then it becomes easier for agency directors, directors of staff development and directors of continuing education to determine what skills and competencies must be developed in workers so that they can accomplish the desired outcomes.

Clearly one of the things in which we need no more training is paper-work. The goals of services coordination do not include sitting at a desk filling out forms. We do need paperwork, but the question is how much and what kind? Values should determine how we spend our time and where we spend our time as service coordinators and case managers. If the major responsibility is integration and community connection, that can not be accomplished sitting behind a desk in an office. It is accomplished by working in the community, by connecting, by facilitating, by building relationships. There are many examples of people who made differences in someone's life by organizing some new relationships with people who were not paid to have that relationship with a person with a developmental disability. That is the challenge. That is the opportunity. I think we know where we want to go.

Service coordinators have the opportunity to be major instruments of change, to assure that people with developmental disabilities truly become members of *our* communities rather than members of special communities.

References

Harris, Louis, & Associates, Inc. (1986). *Disabled americans' self-perceptions: Bringing disabled Americans into the mainstream.* New York, NY: Louis Harris and Associates.

CHAPTER IV

The Search for One-Stop Shopping

by Robert McDonald

Edmonton, where I live, has three major claims to fame. One, it is the capital of the province of Alberta. Two, it is, with Winnipeg, Manitoba, one of the two coldest cities with over a half million people in North America. And three, it is the home of West Edmonton Mall, which is apparently the biggest, and probably the most extravagant, indoor mall on the continent. On a day in January or February, when it is 40 degrees below zero outside, you could go there. You could do all your shopping, have your car repaired, eat at a sidewalk cafe, take in a movie, go skating, visit an amusement park, ride a submarine, and play in the artificial surf of the wave pool - all without going outside. It may be the ultimate in one-stop shopping.

I, personally, find it too big, too noisy, too much a symbol of conspicuous consumption, and I no longer go there. And that's important, too. I have the choice of buying my goods and services locally, from whomever I wish to buy them.

Things are not so easy in my experience for persons with disabilities, or for their families or friends, when they are looking for appropriate services. There are few real choices and certainly no one place I can go, if I wish, to arrange for all the services I need. What I will be discussing is what some advocacy groups in Alberta and British Columbia are doing about that.

Case? Management?

To some extent, Canada and the U.S.A. are two countries separated by a common language (my apologies to Winston Churchill). We have two different political systems, and the differences in terminology can be confusing.

For example, I hear very little about case management or case managers in Alberta. This may be just as well, since the term is redolent of outdated attitudes. No one likes to be thought of as a case, and most people do not want to be managed. If what case managers really do is "service coordination", that sounds better but I have not heard the term used much in Alberta, either.

I do have some experience with case workers in Alberta. I have developed a theory that the title "case worker" refers to people who are working at service coordination but who cannot quite manage. This may be partly due to:

(a) lack of concern. Some people just don't care, but most do. They may however, be frustrated because of:
(b) lack of time. "Case" loads are much too great. Workers may also be hampered by:
(c) lack of skills. This can usually be corrected. What is more difficult to change is:
(d) lack of authority. Case workers are low people on the totem pole. Ultimately, their salaries and their jobs depend more on pleasing their supervisors than on pleasing those people that they are there, in theory, to serve. He who "pays the piper" will sooner or later call the tune.

If persons with disabilities and their families are to be adequately served, more of the power and more of the money, which is the major source of this power, need to be in their hands. What those advocacy groups that I will be talking about are proposing to do, is to put the control of service planning and coordination into the hands of the consumers.

My involvement in this movement began with a workshop which I helped to organize in February, 1985. Representatives of local advocacy groups and service providers were brought together to analyze the present system and to propose ways to improve it. We knew that Alberta Social Services was in the process of putting together a five-year plan for Rehabilitation Services, and we wanted to be prepared to participate whether or not we were invited to do so. We called it Project Blueprint.

This was the first time, to my knowledge, that groups concerned with mental and physical disabilities had even been brought together in this way. It was surprising how much consensus there was about the nature of the problem. We all agreed that there was:

(a) a lack of knowledge about services available and about the rights of disabled persons, both on the part of professionals and of the handicapped persons and their families.
(b) a lack of services, especially in outgoing areas, and inappropriate use of limited resources for bricks and mortar, rather than for direct service to individuals.
(c) a lack of flexibility on programming to fit the strengths and need of individuals. This I call the Procrustean Bed Syndrome. The Greek giant Procrustes had a bed which he said would fit all his "guests." In fact, if his victims were too short, he would stretch them. If they were too tall, he would shorten them. In the modern case, the program is there and if the individual cannot adapt to it, it is the individual's problem. There is always the

choice of moving onto some other program's waiting list, or of
having no service at all.

(d) a lack of continuity and overall coordination which results in
service gaps and in difficulty in gaining access to existing services. A service exists here, another there, still another one
somewhere else. One is federal, one is provincial, another is
private, with little serious effort to make them all mesh together.
All of the services evolved with different criteria for eligibility
(i.e., reasons for rejection). The run-around for individuals and
their families with no one to guide them through the maze is
frustrating, dehumanizing and debilitating.

Even more surprising than the consensus which developed about the
nature of the problem was the degree to which the participants at the
workshop coalesced around two elements of a solution:

(a) Individualized funding, attached somehow to the person being
served and not to a program. This would give the person with
disabilities the power of a consumer in a free market;

(b) A mechanism for overall coordination of services focusing on an
individual, not groups. The original idea was an entity of some
sort which could actively seek out persons in need of service, build
a service system around them, and remain with them, if necessary, from cradle to grave.

But how? Or who? A new government department? A community-based
super agency? Visions of bureaucratic nightmares arise. We decided to form
a committee to work it out.

While we were stumbling along in the dark, we heard what the parents
of the Community Living Society of Greater Vancouver were doing. We also
learned of the existence of the independent living movement which had
grown up among person with physical disabilities. There was an Independent Living Center in Calgary, our sister city to the south.

We obtained funding from the Edmonton regional office of Social Services to do some research. The idea was to look closely at both the community
living and independent living models, pick out the elements we liked, and
design a model appropriate for Edmonton. What we found is the following.

Community Living

The Community Living Society of Greater Vancouver is the brain-child of a
group of parents who had children residing at the Woodlands Institution in
the suburbs of the city.

The group originally came together to see what could be done to improve
conditions at Woodlands, but some parents rapidly came to the conclusion
that the best thing they could do for their children was to remove them.

They approached the British Columbia Ministry of Human Resources and received permission to take five individuals from Woodlands and funding to establish them in the community. Those five individuals were not necessarily the most obvious candidates. There was some suspicion that the government chose them in the expectation that the experiment would fail.

It did not. The parents involved were committed and well-motivated. They had a set of values which emphasized the dignity of the individual, and they had a clear idea of the safeguards necessary for successful deinstitutionalization:

(A) A FIXED POINT OF RESPONSIBILITY

This is the Community Living Board, the executive and administrative arm of the Society. From the point of view of the individual entering the community, this fixed point of responsibility is represented by the broker, employed by the board and assigned a number of persons. The broker coordinates the service planning, estimates the cost, negotiates the funding and arranges the services, then re-assesses and rearranges as necessary. The individual remains with the same broker as long as both are associated with the Board.

(B) FOCUS ON THE INDIVIDUAL

All planning is centered on the individual and involves that individual and all key players in his or her life (family, friends, advocates, professionals). The emphasis is on strengths, rather than needs, and on the individual's preferences, desires and dreams. The aim is not to "fix" the individual, but to create an environment where he or she can blossom and develop. It naturally follows that if planning is individualized, funding must be individualized as well.

(C) PERSONAL SUPPORT NETWORK

Every individual served by the Board must have a personal support network. If no natural support network of family and friends exists, the first thing that must be done is to establish one. The members of the personal support network are involved in the planning of services, and provide continual support to the individual as friends, advocates, and monitors. It is a cardinal rule of community living that the members of the personal support network must have access to the individual they are involved with at all times.

Thus, a model has been developed which is individualized, ensures coordination and continuity, and has built-in checks and balances. It has functioned well since 1979; there have been some failures, but not many.

Nonetheless, there are some significant flaws in the system, at present:

(A) LACK OF ACCESS TO GENERIC SERVICES

It was the intention of the founders of the Community Living Society that "hard services" would be provided by community-based agencies. Being unsuccessful in negotiating the kind of services they wanted, they began to buy their own housing (3-person residences are the norm) and later on to set up their own day programs. The Board now has a Living Arrangements arm, and a Day Programs arm with a staff of 40 to 50. These two arms are administratively independent from the brokerage arm of the Board, but the potential for conflict of interests still exists.

(B) LACK OF TRULY INDIVIDUALIZED FUNDING

The Board has never been able to obtain funding from the province on an individualized basis. It receives two block grants from the Ministry of Human Resources —an administrative grant, and a program grant— which it allocates to the individuals it serves. Ultimately, however, an individual who is not happy with the services provided cannot take his or her money and go somewhere else. As long as this situation exists, he or she is not really in the driver's seat.

(C) RESTRICTED CLIENTELE

The Board has devoted itself over the years to bringing residents of the Woodland institution, all of whom are persons with mental disabilities, back to the community. It has tried one unsuccessful experiment with persons in the community who had never been institutionalized, but has never tried to serve persons with other types of disabilities.

These shortcomings are addressed by the second model which we studied closely, that of the Calgary Association for Independent Living.

Independent Living

The independent living movement arose in the United States as persons with physical disabilities began to organize themselves into advocacy groups. Independent living seems to mean a lot of things to different people, but it generally refers to the empowering of individuals to take control of their own lives, to live autonomously and to participate fully in society. Adherents of this movement see themselves as consumers seeking the same rights as other consumers in the market place.

In Canada, an independent living organization is defined as one which is consumer-controlled, cross-disability, non-profit, and which promotes integration and full participation. Their functions should be to provide information and referral, peer counseling and advocacy, and to encourage the development and improvement of services in general. The Calgary Association for Independent Living concentrates on brokerage. As in the Vancouver community living model, the focus is on the individual, but to a greater degree. The broker works for the individual, not the society, and is involved only to the extent that the individual wishes. The broker may only provide information. He or she may also help in defining the services needed, in preparing the cost estimates, and in negotiating the funding and the service agreements, but only if the individual being served wants it. The importance of personal support networks is also recognized and the broker will facilitate the setting up of such a network, if asked to do so.

The Association provides no "hard" services and insists on individualized funding. It will not accept block program funding. This has been a problem. The only readily available source of individualized funding is a provincial program called Assured Income for the Severely Handicapped (AISH), which generally provides only basic living costs. The Association has a cross-disability, zero-rejection policy. The only constraint on this is the priority given to preventing unwanted institutionalization and to assisting persons to leave institutions.

This model adheres absolutely to the principle of individual choice, refuses specialization on the basis of labels and strictly separates service planning and coordination from service provision. It is a model which has been used mainly with persons labeled as "mentally alert," and in my experience, represents a real challenge to the families of persons with mental disabilities, where the "dignity of risk" *presents* much more of a risk. Realistically, in the case of persons with severe mental disabilities, choices will have to be made by the members of their personal support networks. But the members of these networks need to be constantly challenged to seek out and to respect the preferences of the individual with whom they are concerned.

Where do we go from here?

What is still missing is:

(A) A MODEL DESIGNED TO SUIT THE NEEDS OF INFANTS, AND YOUNG CHILDREN WITH DISABILITIES

If families have the support they need to keep their children at home and to integrate them into local schools and community organizations, there will never be a need to try to fit their children back into the community later on.

(B) A MECHANISM FOR INDIVIDUALIZED FUNDING

Government and private agencies have a vested interest in maintaining block funding for programs and services. From the government's point of view, block funding is simpler to administer and makes it easier to impose artificial limits on expenditures. Private service-providing agencies tend to see individualized funding as a threat to their financial security, since their overall revenues would be dependent on how many people they could attract to their services. Both government and private agencies would be forced to do their planning from the bottom up rather than from the top down. In short, they would lose power. Nonetheless, there are precedents, e.g., individual grants for pre-school education of children with severe or multiple disabilities; the Assured Income for the Severely Handicapped program referred to above; and the Handicapped Children's Services grants available from Alberta Social Services to parents of children with disabilities who need financial support. In addition, our government now appears to have committed itself to individualized funding for persons being moved from large institutions into the community. The challenge is to expand these existing sources of individualized funding.

(C) A MECHANISM FOR IDENTIFICATION AND REFERRAL

A disability, actual or potential, may be detected at different stages in life— at birth or infancy, at school age, or even later as a result of illness or injury. When this happens, the individuals involved and their families need moral support and information about their condition and about available services. In Alberta, no one has the responsibility to see that this kind of vital support is provided. All too often, people are left entirely to their own devices. With luck, they may stumble onto someone who can help, or they may not. It seems to me that the public health system is in the best position to provide information and referral. The usual excuse for not taking on this role is that some sort of violation of individual rights might be involved (translation: we do not want to create a demand that we would then have to fill). Until this problem is solved, advocacy groups and brokerage agencies will not be able to function optimally—they cannot serve people who do not know they exist.

The Vision and the Reality

My vision of the future is for a multitude of independent brokerage agencies in more or less free competition. They would be run by persons with disabilities and/or their families and advocates. They might receive core funding from public or private sources for administrative costs. The rest of their funding would come from the individuals they would serve. They would be prohibited from offering any hard services, except perhaps on a temporary, emergency basis.

Hard services would be provided by another network of agencies, public or private, functioning on similar principles.

The reality, at present, is that various groups around the province are in the process of establishing brokerage agencies. The government set up an office in January, 1986, with powers to approve and fund community-living projects. (It is called the Bureau for Independent Living, thereby adding to the confusion). Some service-providing agencies have jumped on the band wagon by developing internal brokerage structures. One such agency, at least, has already received approval and funding for a project, even though the Bureau for Independent Living has yet to make public any criteria, standards or procedures. One can only hope that everything will be sorted out sooner rather than later. In the meantime, the only thing to do is to forge ahead by whatever means possible.

P.S.—to Case Managers

Some of the ideas expressed above may seem threatening to you. Remain calm. Your role is (or ought to be) to enable, to facilitate and to empower persons with handicaps to take control of their lives to the very greatest extent possible. If you are good at it, nothing in my vision of the future need worry you. In fact, if my vision becomes reality, you will be all the more free to do your job as you would want to do it.

Update

Since this presentation, the Edmonton Community Living Society, of which Robert McDonald is a charter member, has been created. It has developed, under contract with the Community Resource Management Branch of Alberta Social Services, a model for an independent brokerage service in Edmonton, has received funding and is now in operation as a brokerage agency.

Copies of the document *Edmonton Community Living Society: Proposal for Brokerage Service*, Edmonton, June 30, 1987, may be requested from:

William Winship, Manager
Community Rehabilitation Programs
Alberta Social Services
Edmonton Region
11748 Kingsway Avenue
Edmonton, Alberta C5G OX5

CHAPTER V

Case Management Through the Life Cycle

by Betty Pendler

bstract

This chapter is a very personal and intimate account of a parent about the life cycle of her daughter who has Down Syndrome. It begins with speculation about what their lives would have been like IF they had had a case manager beginning with the time she was told about her daughter's condition. Periods of crisis are highlighted, and in an honest and forthright manner, she describes her early emotions.

Many critical periods are discussed in detail including encounters with the service system. The impact of society's attitudes all along the way is dramatically described, as are the need for early direction and guidance, and the need for changing attitudes.

Needs are highlighted in the areas of advocacy for the parent in the school system, recreational needs, respite services, and other areas. She describes in a humorous manner her attempts to let go and teach her daughter how to travel alone, and describes her ambivalent feeling about residential placement and the successful adjustment both she and her daughter ultimately make. Her feelings on the subject of sexuality are clearly and honestly expressed.

The author ends with the need for parents to have guidance to accept the new directions of independent living, employment in the community, and self-advocacy for the young adult, and concludes that a good case manager must anticipate parents' needs and thus give them direction to alleviate the hardships and heartbreaks that she herself encountered.

Discovery

What if I had had a knowledgeable, sensitive, and caring case manager from the moment Lisa, my daughter who has Down Syndrome, was born; how different would my life have been? Would I have been spared the scars of what I call "my battle with myself and society" as a result of having a child who is different? I propose to let you, the reader, decide as I unfold to you the entire story of my life.

I married late in life (37), and it was a first marriage for both my husband and me. At that time I had three girl friends, all of whom married late in life, and all of whom gave birth to healthy, bouncing babies. Therefore, it was with great excitement and expectation, when at the age of 39, I became pregnant. At that time I had never heard of the term "mongoloid" which was the prevalent word for Down Syndrome, nor was I aware of the statistics of older women having a first child born with Down Syndrome. Therefore, on August 27, 1955, there was much joy and excitement in the Pendler family when Lisa was born. However, my girl friends and my sister-in-law who came to the hospital and saw Lisa through the glass door of the nursery apparently had noted immediately the facial characteristics, and it is only in retrospect that I recall wondering why they were not as excited as I.

Human nature being what it is, one tends not to remember what one does not want to, so again, it was only in retrospect that I recall the obstetrician telling me that my pediatrician would talk to me. I also recall now the pediatrician telling me during the first three monthly visits, "Let's see how she is doing next month." However, the most insistent of my three girl friends kept subtly suggesting that I see her doctor when I complained about Lisa's slow sucking reflex. I was already beginning to have a gnawing feeling, which I could have done without—had someone spoken to me in a kind, knowledgeable, and sensitive manner immediately in the hospital. My husband scoffed at the suggestion that I see another doctor and proposed that we confront our pediatrician at our next appointed visit. I wished I had listened to him as I would have been spared a devastating experience. As a caution to wives—sometimes our husbands do know what is best for us!

My girl friend drove me to her doctor, so sure that she was doing the right thing. There ensued one of the most heart-rending and devastating emotional experiences in my entire life. This very cold, "professional" pediatrician examined Lisa, holding her by the scruff of her neck like a plucked chicken, and proceeded to use medical terms, which I had never heard of, and then pointed to the significant characteristics of "mongolism", such as the shape of her neck, the formation of her hands and eyes. He immediately suggested that since she was a girl, and I would encounter many problems with her, I should go home and discuss with my husband the possibility of placement.

Need you be surprised at my trauma, since at the very worst, I was expecting him to tell me that perhaps she had some problem with her tongue that was interfering with her sucking; certainly nothing like this! So where was someone for me to cling to at that moment? My friend drove me home in a state of complete shock. When my husband arrived at home, I related the story, amid tears and hysteria. We talked and cried and talked again. We even discussed the prospect of placement, but both agreed that we would give it time, and should it appear that Lisa could not function in society for lack of service, or either one of us could not take it emotionally, then we would face that issue.

I recall so vividly Mac's first question to me: "Betty, we did not know yesterday that Lisa was mentally retarded. Tell me, is she less precious to you today than she was yesterday?" I am fortunate to be a person who is very honest with myself (and others), and perhaps because I come from a middle class background, my immediate answer to him was, "yes, d... it". There went my dreams of having a college-bound daughter.

The next few nights as we talked about the coldness, the brutality, and inhumane manner of that doctor, and about the possibility of placement and that horrible phrase, "putting away," we also talked about where to go and whom to call. I could see my husband agonizing as much as I. I cannot help speculating now how valuable a third, objective, sensitive person would have helped during this painful period before we returned to our original pediatrician.

Be that as it may, we finally did see our pediatrician, who was very annoyed at me because I did not trust him enough to come to him first. He told us that he was fully prepared to tell us that his suspicion was confirmed, and that he planned to tell me all about the condition and refer me to the Association for Retarded Citizens. To his defense, I must add that even in the hospital records they had a question mark next to the word "mongoloid" because of familial features - I have slanted eyes and my husband has a short neck.

Our joy and excitement ended when Lisa was three months old, and I had to come to full grips with the knowledge that I have a child who is different. It is at this time that parents need some sense of sanity and balance in their lives. Some sense of perspective has to be created to help us reach the adjustments that will enable us to view ourselves as parents and our child as a child. We need some place to go in confidence to help us shape our future.

There ensued a flood of emotions which hit me everyday in varying degrees. 1 remember how my husband, Mac, looked at me in horror when I confessed to him that when I was giving Lisa a bath in the bassinet how tempted I was to fill it up to the top with water, or how I was tempted to throw the both of us into the subway pit as I brought her to the doctor for subsequent examinations. Can the reader envision the horror and fear of parents when these thoughts run through their mind: the fear of being punished by God, the inexorable guilt every time you kiss or hug your child? I had to wait almost two years to find that these emotions are quite common when I chanced upon some literature on the subject. There was an article by Wolfsenberger (1970) who at that time was working in the Kansas State School and did a research study on parents' reactions to the impact of having a child who is mentally retarded. He says:

> There is an infinite variety of initial or early reactions, alarm,
> ambivalence, anger, anguish, anxiety, avoidance, bewilderment,
> bitterness, confusion, death wish, depression, despair, disbelief,
> envy, fear, frustration, grief, guilt, hopelessness, helplessness,
> impulse to destroy the child, mourning, over-identification, projec-
> tions, rejection, self-blame, self-pity, shame, shock, trauma (p. 330).

I submit that at one time or another I experienced every one of the aforementioned emotions; I was very jealous of my three girl friends, not wishing them to have had a child who is handicapped, but the "why-me?" syndrome lingered for a long time. I have already alluded to some of the other emotions.

It was a few years later when I returned to school that I read an article by Solnit (1961) about the mourning process. He talked about how a parent mourns over the birth of a child who is handicapped as if the child were dead, until a resocialization period sets in. He goes on to say there is no time for working through the loss of the desired child before there is a demand to invest in the new and handicapped child as a love object, and here is where the physician or a social worker's responsibility to facilitate this process is needed. Did I have to wait three years to learn this? Indeed, a case manager could have taken on the role that Solnit describes.

Further, in the beginning, we needed advice on how to tell the grandparents, friends, and neighbors; how to talk about it without breaking down. It seems quite ironic that it was we, the parents of the child who is handicapped, who had to put our friends who were brave enough to visit us, at ease with *their* discomfort! That was another role in which we could have used guidance. Perhaps I am asking too much of a case manager, but as I am reviewing my life to pinpoint difficult periods, I recall this issue as not an easy one, and one we had to deal with and overcome.

Mac and I both tussled with our emotions. We were determined to follow the philosophy of William James to act "as if a thing were so." We were determined to try to live as normal a life as possible within the reality of the situation. My inner anger never left me, but it was this constructive anger that gave me the impetus to start the ball rolling, and which also began what I called my "battle with society": the encompassing community, neighbors, friends, professionals, and society-at-large. I became my own case manager by immediately writing a letter to the American Medical Association deploring the lack of education on the part of doctors in speaking to parents. I am not sure much has changed, but at least I felt better getting it off my chest! I did join the local chapter, New York City Association for Retarded Citizens, which at that time did not have too many services but did have parent meetings. I recall with what utter amazement I viewed the smiles on the faces of the other parents at these meetings thinking, "How is that possible?" It was there that I learned it was parents, not professionals, who became the case managers for us new parents. Little did I know that I was to follow a rewarding life of case managing for hundreds of other parents.

After a few years, I was anxious to try for a second baby. I confess I had a very hard time convincing my husband. Although genetic counseling was not prevalent in those days, I certainly could have used someone to talk to both of us. However, I succeeded in convincing him, and on June 26, 1958, Paul was born after nine months of the most apprehensive pregnancy any mother has encountered. It was during this period, after Paul was born, that many well-meaning friends talked about this being a good time to place Lisa because of the possible impact she would have on her "normal" brother. The comments were sometimes subtle, sometimes brutally frank, until you were ready to burst and tell them "mind your own business." However, by this time, I felt I had someone to talk to in the parent organization, and of course had decided to go on with our lives. This was one added pressure, however, I could have done without.

Finding Appropriate Services

I have always maintained that to the degree that society accepts a person who is different, the impact on that person's parents is lessened. I wonder how much has changed even today. In those days, I found myself taking Lisa to the playground less and less because I could not stand the open stares of children and parents, and the overt actions of parents literally "yanking" their child out of the sandbox when they noticed Lisa with her obviously different features. Interestingly enough, I finally switched to a playground frequented by people with few financial advantages and there I had no problem. However, until I discovered that, the pain inside of me increased. Where was someone to help me talk about how to handle this situation? It wasn't until much later I learned that many people fear that which they do not understand. Their reaction to the unknown is either ignoring it, laughing at it, or just being unkind.

It is hard for us to realize how diverse and fragmented services are, as there are some agencies that may deal competently with one aspect of the child's problem, but know nothing about organizations and groups dealing with other aspects. For example, there are physicians who are at a loss to refer a parent to the non-medical community resources, and family agencies that do not know about the specific problems of the child who is handicapped, as you will see from the next crisis in my life.

Because of my involvement in the local chapter of ARC, I was able to get limited services such as speech lessons at that time. I do not mean to devalue the services obtained, but I still recall the early professional attitudes displayed. The helping professions were only slightly better than the well-intentioned friends and playground mothers. I submit that many professionals, even at this late date, communicate in a way that negates their ability to be of any effective help. Fortunately, I do sincerely believe that this is changing somewhat, as professionals are learning to talk WITH parents instead of TO parents.

When Lisa was three years old and Paul only thirteen months, my husband passed away, and it was hard to find a professional who could refer me to the proper source. The typical social worker was able to attempt to help me with my grief, but admittedly knew nothing about mental retardation. The social worker at the ARC tried feebly to help me with my grief. I have a vivid recollection of having been referred to a family service organization by a good social worker at the clinic where Lisa was getting speech lessons, with the hope that I would be able to get a homemaker. However, this well-intentioned professional, who was very Freudian-oriented, insisted on talking to me about other issues, such as why I married so late in life, and what was the relationship my parents had. He gave the explanation that he had to know me as a total person before he could counsel me on my grief, or even handle the hard issues such as the need for a homemaker or how to handle my limited resources. Through lack of knowledge in the field of mental retardation, he even suggested that to ease my burden, perhaps it would be wise to think of having Lisa placed. Obviously he turned out not to be too helpful, either with my grief, or with handling Lisa. By the time he delved into my past life, I had succeeded on my own to enroll Lisa in a day care nursery about which you will hear somewhat later in this narrative.

Somehow, I survived, largely through the kindness and loving attention of the Barbery family, wonderful Spanish-speaking neighbors in my building who accepted Lisa completely, assisted in my baby-sitting, and gave me what is now called "respite." It was then that I was able to go to school to pursue my college education and go back to work. Today when people compliment me on what a good job I appear to have done with both of my children, I never fail to say that I never could have done it without this wonderful family's support.

However, even with their help, I was still to encounter my battle with society as I searched for programs for Lisa so that I could go back to full-time, gainful employment and pay my neighbors for their loving services. It is true that today there are such programs as Head Start and other early intervention programs, but at that time I was forced to make the rounds on my own. I contacted every conceivable agency, church, synagogue, and community center. Speaking about society's attitudes, I can vividly recall the body language of the many professionals and administrators who moved slightly backward when I mentioned by daughter was mentally retarded, after which I received either a flat refusal, or polite excuses such as, "although they had no objection, they feared the reactions of other parents." How much easier my life would have been if a third objective person could have made these rounds for me, and eliminated the horrendous experience of such overt rejection.

Society's attitude is so subtle that even professionals are not aware of what I call institutionalized prejudice toward the person who is different. I wish to relate briefly what I refer to as my "yellow pad" story. After many months of searching, I finally found one summer school program run by a local community center which appeared to be interested in having someone who was "different" in their program. This was surely a far-sighted professional long before mainstreaming had been known. I could not believe my ears and recall repeating the fact that my daughter was handicapped. I remember asking her what I should tell the other children about Lisa. She responded that I need not worry about the children, rather, it is the parents who are a problem. She calmly told me that she was going to explain to them that just as God made some children who don't hear well, or see well, so they made some children like Lisa who do not understand, and assured me that she would handle the parents. She did request that I sit in the back of the classroom for the first week because she knew the teacher would be apprehensive. I am happy to say that this was a very successful experience, and we all agreed that both Lisa and the other children benefited.

This experience gave me courage to approach the local day care nursery, which is funded by the Department of Social Service. I approached the director, who happened to know the program director of the summer program. She appeared to be quite amenable and approached the teacher who would be in charge. However, she explained to me that final approval had to come from the Department of Social Service. I was to bring Lisa for observation the following Monday.

I brought Lisa to the nursery where everyone was playing in the playground. The social worker was seated—with a yellow pad. I did not know then what I know now: that many people who have poor speech often touch in order to communicate. Lisa went over to a little girl and touched her. Obviously the social worker interpreted this as scratching her. I was quick to notice that the social worker wrote something on that yellow pad, and my stomach skipped a beat. Lisa, however, being as sociable as I am, went over to another little girl and touched her. Again a notation was made on the yellow pad. I submit that the Kaopectate industry gets rich on us parents because of the silent bland faces of professionals as they write on yellow pads, without explaining what it is they are writing.

Indeed, as we went into the office with the director, the social worker expressed her fear that Lisa had exhibited aggressive behavior, and that she was concerned about the reaction of the parents of the other children. I tried hard to control my emotions at this comment, but was relieved by the attitude of the director who explained that since the teacher did not object, perhaps they should accept Lisa for a trial period. This is what happened and, needless to say, Lisa did very well...but, that is not the point of my story. The following year Paul became three years of age, which made him eligible for day care nursery. Since I was so anxious to relieve my wonderful neighbors of the burden of baby care, as I had returned to work, I brought Paul to this same day care nursery.

Once again at the playground, there was a social worker, a different one of course, but she had a yellow pad on her lap. Paul, who was a bouncing, healthy, chubby boy saw the jungle gym in the playground. I recall this day so vividly (25 years later— just as I recall the incident of the suburban doctor holding Lisa by the scruff of her neck), and saw Paul literally PUSH a little boy as he rushed to the jungle gym—and NOTHING WAS WRITTEN ON THE YELLOW PAD. I think I can rest my case about unconscious attitudes all along the way, and the need for someone to talk to parents about this— which we never had. Space does not permit my relating numerous other incidents of similar impact, but I will mention a few.

When it was apparent that Lisa needed some kind of dental service, just finding a dentist to take care of a child who was handicapped was difficult. I had a personal, close friend who was a dentist. He was very honest with me when he confessed that since he had no experience with this population, he would rather not treat Lisa. I know today the situation is different, as our local ARC has a resource for such a service. But where could I go then to get this information? Lisa by this time was enrolled in the special classes in the public school system, and this particular school had dental services for the entire school. When I inquired as to why the special classes were not getting this service, the nurse blithely responded, "These children don't sit still, so we can't handle them". By that time I had learned to successfully control my inner anger at such phrases as "these children", but my adrenalin did go up. I calmly explained that my daughter was entitled to this service, and impressed the nurse with the use of some names of important people in the school system. No doubt she felt that she better not tussle with this parent and consented to examine Lisa's class. The following week I received a note from her telling me what a "brave soldier" Lisa was after having an extraction. Needless to say, I hastened to write her and suggested that she change her mind about "these children"— another indication of unconscious attitudes, which in this case, led to a lack of service as well.

Before long I was confronted with the sibling situation when Paul began to ask me why Lisa talked funny. Fortunately, I was able to explain this to him, using the explanation that the director from the first summer program Lisa attended used. He appeared to accept that. I knew in my heart of hearts, that even at age five, he experienced the same sinking sensation that I do when we walked on the street and people stared. I remember his coming to me telling me he was going to punch our four-year-old next door neighbor in the nose because he made fun of his sister. While I praised him at the time, somewhat later I tried to explain to him how people don't always understand, and that it was all right if he felt funny inside, as even I felt funny inside. I was aware even then that we could have used guidance in handling this situation. Fortunately for me, because of my honesty, I was very open with him and gave him permission to be honest with his ambivalent emotions.

I know there is no doubt that having a child who is handicapped has to affect the entire family structure. No matter how much we, as parents, think we are living normally, there has to be some effect on every member, but it need not necessarily be a damaging one. I used the word "retarded" quite freely from a very early age in front of both Lisa and Paul. My son knew that I was very busy going to meetings to help people who are mentally retarded. I know that eventually Paul too would understand that society has to change it's attitudes. However, I worked hard not only to give him freedom to feel ambivalent about his sister, but also to try to make him have positive feelings about her. I received unexpected help from a well-known TV program called "Lassie" about a boy and his dog.

One night the three of us were watching this program in which the little boy asked his mother if Lassie can catch beavers, to which the mother replied, "No, dear." The boy looked crestfallen, but then the mother went on to say, "You see, dear, even though Lassie can't catch beavers, he can do other things; everyone and everything has its own special value." I quickly picked up on this beautiful phrase, called it to Paul's attention, and explained that this was like Lisa, who may not talk as well as he, but still has her own special values. I was not aware that, at the age of 5, he absorbed this. However, that summer, the three of us went away for a two-week vacation at a family camp run by a social agency, and I overheard a little boy in the cabin next door telling Paul that his sister talked funny. I saw through the window Paul stamping his little foot and saying righteously, "Well, she is like Lassie, she has her own special values." I think I could have used more than this TV program to help me with the sibling issues, I am sure.

The entire area of public school education for the child who is handicapped could be made easier with the intervention of a case manager. Prior to Public Law 94-142, it proved to be quite traumatic with waiting lists, attitudes on the part of principals, teachers, and other parents in regular classes. One more indication that not only were our children outsiders, but we as parents were forced into this category for our very efforts to survive this battle. It is very difficult to attend the PTA meetings and never hear any concern for the problems of children in the special classes. It was only when the more active parents began to organize the parents of children in the special classes that we even had a chance to express these needs. Things have changed! I am happy to report that our local chapter of the Association for Retarded Citizens has a paid educational advocate to whom a case manager could refer a parent in order to help the parent get the required curriculum and other services that I didn't have. In fact, I recall in the early days of Lisa's education that I was literally afraid to ask the teacher how she was getting along, for fear that she would give me negative reports and not keep her in the program.

With the advent of P.L. 94-142, there is a great need for parents to know how to use the empowerment they have under this legislation. We need advice on how to use these new-found rights. We have to learn how to refuse the often-used statement by professionals that parents are too emotional and too closely involved to be effective advocates. Some of us have to learn how to reply in the proper manner and to explain, because we are so closely and personally involved, that is precisely why we can make such effective advocates. Therefore, we could use guidance in fostering our confidence in our ability to effect change. There are far too many parents who still feel they do not have enough expert knowledge to tell the teacher what should go into their child's Individual Education Plan (IEP). I am grateful for the many parent advocacy centers that are doing such a wonderful job due to recent legislation which Senator Lowell Weicker fought hard for. Still, someone has to direct the parent to these excellent resources.

Recreational opportunities became another stumbling block since I could not take Lisa and Paul to the same recreational programs, even in terms of a summer camp. While I could find an inexpensive agency camp for Paul, it was very difficult in those days to find one who would accept Lisa for a sleepaway experience. Eventually, through the social worker at our local ARC, I did locate such a camp. How much better it would have been if there were someone who could have anticipated the needs that were going to face me ahead of time and eliminate so much anguish on my part.

Not only was it important for me and for Lisa to find recreational programs, which were very few in those days, but also in order for me to have a relationship with Paul, I needed time to do things with him alone. This was difficult since there were no programs for Lisa to attend. I think in any normal family relationship a parent should give each sibling private time (handicapped or not). Therefore, the subject of respite soon reared its ugly head. Had Lisa been able to have respite for a weekend, Paul and I could have had our time together. I think I need not remind anyone that this much needed service is a problem in the human service system even today. Even in my time, an innovative case manager might have arranged a parent network or some other helpful situation.

Growing Up

It is not my intention to paint a dark, discouraging picture of my life. In fact, because of my strength, my positive attitude, and my involvement in the parent organization, Lisa and I had a relatively stable life. I was able to go back to college, as well. However, I found that I, like most parents of children who are handicapped, tended to be overprotective. Most parents, even more than I, because we were forced to be outsiders, did not socialize with their former friends. They did not expose their child who was handicapped to more normalizing situations and spent an inordinate amount of time with their son or daughter who was developmentally disabled, thus falling into the trap of becoming dependent on the dependency. There is such a danger of this for all of us, which could, perhaps in some part, be somewhat alleviated through the intervention of good counseling very early in this dependent relationship. Overprotection, under the guise of love for our son or daughter, can be quite insidious, and we parents need someone to call this to our attention. But where and from whom were we to get such guidance?

Letting go is not easy for parents in general, and certainly much more difficult for parents who have children with handicapping conditions. We can always use the rationale (or excuse) that precisely because our child is handicapped, he or she needs us all the more. I remember quite well the tortures I went through when I knew that I had to teach Lisa how to travel. I had to keep reminding myself that I had to do this despite my anxiety. Very often our overprotection is more to alleviate our own anxieties than it is to help our son or daughter. I was honest enough to realize this. I was aware of the system that the New York City Board of Education used to travel-train the young adults who were in their special classes and decided that I would attempt to do the same thing.

Lisa was nearly twenty years old, and I was still escorting her to her Saturday and Sunday afternoon programs. I knew that the time had come for me to teach her how to face the perils of the New York City subway system, the subway riders, the stalled trains and the need not to talk to strangers. It was with much trepidation that I began the program, although I was convinced in my own mind that she and her friend Susie, whom I had been escorting for at least three years, seemed to know the way. They always knew exactly at which stops to get off to make the change of trains and on which street to turn to get to the program. I explained to them that since they were so grown up, I was going to teach them how to do it on their own. They were both so pleased indicating that they knew already! I did explain to them that for a few weeks we would leave the house together, but I would sit in another section of the train. They both again reassured me that they knew and said, "You'll see". Well, see I did! I was pleasantly surprised to notice on these few trips that, indeed, both girls got up at the right stop to leave and proudly turned back to look at me. I'm wondering if secretly I wasn't a bit disappointed that they seemed to know it so well - and no longer needed me.

Finally the day came for their first experience of actually traveling alone, and my first experience of almost dying a thousand deaths as I followed them, but this time, without their knowing it. I knew that in the New York City School training program, when they considered the trainee ready to travel on his or her own, someone - not the usual trainer- followed. The trainer would tell the students that on this day they were to be on their own, but unbeknown to them, the follower would check to make sure they made their destination.

Since I could not arrange for a stranger to play this role, I attempted to do it myself and hoped I would not be observed. Secrecy is certainly possible in the New York City subway system since the stations are long enough for me to stand at one end and still be unobserved. Saturday morning arrived and Lisa and Susie proudly walked off towards the subway. I bade them good-bye, explaining to them that when they returned I might not be home, but would return shortly thereafter. As soon as they left the house, I donned a hat (I never wear hats as a general rule) and borrowed a coat from my neighbor, a bright red one, a color that I would never wear. I hoped that even if I were noticed from a distance, my disguise would assure Lisa that this person could not be her mother.

I rushed to the subway stairs, just a few minutes after Lisa and Susie did. I wanted to make sure that I would catch the same train. I saw them get on, and I pushed and shoved in order to get into the third or fourth car beyond theirs. Pushing and shoving is quite common in the New York subways so this behavior was not so bizarre. The trip was uneventful and it was easy for me to see them through the crowds. I was quite thrilled to see the two girls reassuring themselves about which staircase to take and at which stop to get off. I was able to see that they did, indeed, get to their program and they were completely unaware of me. Four hours later I had to begin my sleuthing again. At dismissal time I stood around the corner from the center where the program was being held. I saw them getting ready to leave, so I scurried down a different staircase and hid beneath the stairwell. I was so intent on being on guard and unseen that it did not occur to me that I might be considered rather peculiar as I stalked in and out of the stairwell, and no doubt received plenty of strange looks from the other subway riders. Finally, I heard their voices, again repeating the directions of where to get off, and where to make the changes for the second stop. I knew then that I had been underestimating them all this time.

I remained under the stairwell until the train came, and to my horror, the first train that came into the station was not the usual one (the first of my thousand deaths). What should I do— should I come clean and caution them not to take this train, or wait and see if they would go in and then quickly run out and shout, "Save those children!" I began to walk backwards so that I would not be recognized, and noticed two women looking at me quizzically as I hid behind another person. I breathed a sigh of relief when I heard them tell each other that this was not the "D" train, and they held hands and stood firm. Apparently my constant repetition during the period I was training them paid off. However, they still had to make another change, and there is always the chance in New York City that passengers are asked to change trains in mid-stream; the pit of my stomach was still churning away. The next change the girls had to make was at a very crowded station, and I almost lost them. I pushed myself through the crowds with a soft "pardon me", and finally saw them enter the right train. Since I had told them that I would not be at home when they got there, I did not take the chance of getting off at the same stop for fear of being spotted. I rode one more stop and arrived home fifteen minutes later. They were both beaming with pride and a sense of accomplishment as they both said, "We made it." I expressed pleasure and surprise and relief, as I had made it, too. However, once again I suggest that perhaps early on I could have been directed to an experienced travel-trainer, as well as advice about the fact that Lisa was far more prepared for independence than I was. I realized that I used the excuse for too long that strangers would take advantage of her, or that she could not manage on her own because I was not ready to "let go". Surely we parents can use courses in "letting go" very early on. This is not easy, and indeed Lisa did get lost a few times. I have to remind myself that my behavior should not be motivated by my desire to lessen my anxiety but by what is best for Lisa.

Coming into Adulthood

We have now reached the point where Lisa has completed her education through the Division of Special Education and is enrolled in the sheltered workshop sponsored by our local ARC. She is feeling quite independent. As you can imagine, by this time I am no longer a young parent. I get a gnawing feeling as I think of what is going to happen to Lisa when I am gone. Is it fair to give Paul such an awesome responsibility?

The next problems facing me were looking into residential services, the need for guardianship, and life planning. We all have a deep concern that our son or daughter will have someone to look after his or her emotional needs after we are gone, a sort of parental surrogate. The fear of what will happen to our son or daughter after we are gone is a constant specter that haunts us in spite of the services that are in place. There are all kinds of legal arrangements and corporate guardianships that parents need to have guidance in, so here is one more role for a case manager.

One other area that parents never face quite fully or honestly is the entire subject of sexuality as related to a person who is developmentally disabled. Professor Sol Gordon once said that it has taken us years to convince people that most parents and professionals can handle the fact that people with developmental disabilities are human, but cannot handle the sexual aspect. The over-protection syndrome weighs heavily on the entire subject of sexuality, particularly if it is a female who is developmentally disabled. The fear of pregnancy and the fear of exploitation often inhibit the development of a healthy sexual attitude on the part of either parents or young adults. Parents can use guidance very early on for their conflicting feelings about the subject, for instance, of masturbation. It is hard for them to realize that this can be a healthy activity contributing to the physical and emotional well being of their child. Here again, the conflicting and ambivalent feelings which besiege parents of children who are developmentally disabled could be alleviated with early guidance or direction to a parent support group on the subject. Once more, I recall my early unfounded fears of how I was going to explain the subject of menstruation to Lisa. If we had someone who could anticipate this need on the part of the parents before it occurs, our anguishing moments could be very much alleviated. Parents need help in getting over the myth that people who are handicapped are asexual or uncontrollable, and therefore we must ignore their sexual feelings. The question should not be whether our child should have sex information, but when, how, and by whom—and for this, we parents need guidance and direction.

It was time for me to look at residential services very seriously, and I knew that it was important for both Lisa and myself to be ready. Both the adult with developmental disabilities and the parent need to have a readiness program. This is one more example where good guidance is necessary to handle the separation problem. Parents renew their sense of guilt as they view the "putting away" syndrome and once again go through a tumultuous period. Lisa has been living in a group home for eight years now and is extremely happy. However, as I look back at my behavior, even though I considered myself as one of those parents who worked hard to prepare Lisa for independence and separation, I saw instances of holding back and resistance to letting her go. I had begun to take Lisa to visit various group homes run by the various voluntary agencies in New York City, and it was she who said to me, albeit in broken speech, "I can hardly wait to move and get rid of my mother." Once again those ambivalent feelings loomed. Lisa was traveling more or less independently of me and I no longer had to pick her up for programs, so I did not feel that she was holding me back. I knew that Lisa, like all other young men and women in their twenties, would want to move out and be on her own. As independent as I have tried to make my daughter become, I believe that I still did not really want to relinquish my role as the protective loving mother. There is no doubt in my mind now that this move for Lisa at the age of 23 was the wisest, and most correct and necessary move for us all.

As the movement towards group homes and independent apartment clusters grew, I was able to see first hand the growth and development of the young men and women away from their protective parents. I knew I owed it to Lisa and to Paul to file an application with the various agencies. I had soul-searched my feelings and knew this was the right thing to do. I wanted Lisa settled during my lifetime so that I could assist her with any necessary adjustment. Yet, I confess to all that the several applications sat on my desk at home for one whole year, and here I was giving advice to parents on the dignity of risk and letting go. I was immobile for a whole year, and realized that I should have started to think about the positive aspects of her moving out when Lisa was as young as fifteen or sixteen. Perhaps this ambivalent feeling would not have assailed me at this point but would have been resolved at a much earlier time. Finally I did file the application and heaved a sigh of relief when I was told there was a year's waiting list.

However, the day finally came when I was told Lisa would enter the group home in February. She began making visits to the facility to get acquainted. It was interesting to hear the reaction of some of my neighbors when I informed them of my decision to have Lisa move out on her own, but they all perceived it as my "putting her away" and gently chided me. Needless to say these comments did not help my own already ambivalent feelings about whether I was doing the right thing. I constantly had butterflies in my stomach. I recall very vividly one evening when Lisa, Paul, and I were having dinner just prior to the date when Lisa would be moving. Both of them were having a good-natured joust with one another when Paul looked at me and voiced the exact thought that was going through my mind. He said, "Why does Lisa have to move out? We have so much togetherness!" For a moment I almost agreed with him, but I had to remind myself as to whose comfort and happiness I was concerned with and knew that I had to get off this unbalanced end of the see-saw.

I realize that the psychological dynamics of not being ready to let go are so subtle that we parents are not aware of it, but not until it was called to my attention was I aware of how deep-rooted they are. Although Lisa was fairly independent, still, at the age of 22 I had to take her shopping for clothes. Many a Saturday, when I preferred to go to a matinee or a concert with my friends and I had to take her shopping, I reverted to the "why me" syndrome. My three girl friends who had daughters Lisa's age were not bound to give up their Saturdays for shopping as their daughters were easily capable of handling money and buying their own clothes. Therefore, it was with admitted resentment that I performed this task and hoped that my resentment was not evident to Lisa.

Lisa finally moved into the group home, and we were all happy with the decision and the adjustment. Two months after she moved in, the director informed me that since Lisa was going to need lots of new clothes for camp, they would be taking her shopping and wanted a list of items and her sizes. Can you believe my response? A flutter in the pit of my stomach forced me to say, "What do you mean, you are going shopping with her—I LOVE to take her shopping and take her out to lunch!" I blocked out completely those Saturdays that I resented so deeply. The dynamics exhibited here are subtle. It would have been so helpful to have received some guidance.

A Role for the Case Manager

The needs and gaps never end and I see now that Lisa is very happy in her group home of eight young adults. Eventually she will have a need for a greater degree of independent living as well as the need to enter the employment field instead of the more restrictive environment of a workshop. I confess that although I know it is the right direction for her, I am resisting it and am, honestly speaking, quite fearful. Featherstone (1980) mentions that it is very frightening for parents now that the federal government and workshops are pushing for new policies that will send our adult sons and daughters into the community. Many parents object vigorously as we worry about community hostility, or that personal failure will hurt our child, and we worry about the physical danger hidden in the workday world. I hope I will not be one of those parents who object vigorously, but as Featherstone points out, it is understandable that professionals "want to challenge the workers as they see signs of growth" (p. 20). Once again we parents will need to know this long before it happens. If only there were case managers easily available who could not only anticipate this need, but our fear and apprehension, and begin to give us guidance to overcome the fears that ultimately interfere with the growth of our son or daughter.

Parents will need guidance to have faith in the future direction of self-advocacy which is growing rapidly based on the actual performance of persons who are developmentally disabled. These young people, who previously were considered incapable of benefiting from education, are demonstrating in increasing numbers that with a strong support system, they have the capacity for participation in their own planning and programming and can serve on committees. Gold (1972) opened up a new perspective on this subject when he demonstrated how effectively he could teach work skills to individuals once considered totally incapable of any part of a production process. I know that a few years ago this would have been brushed aside as totally unrealistic and confess to my own ambivalent feelings at this point. This is a whole new area for case managers to give us parents faith in our sons and daughters.

I feel that I am beginning to unconsciously define the role of a case manager as one who anticipates in advance all the possible problems and needs of parents and their sons and daughters who are developmentally disabled. Dickman (1985) mentioned in his book, *One Miracle at a Time*, that what is missing is a road map, a sort of dictionary of guidance, where to go and what to do to get to all the services that a child who is developmentally disabled needs. I cannot begin to fathom how such a system can be put into place and still give the parent the opportunity to have choices and options and not feel obligated to accept the services suggested by the case manager. But I will leave that up to people in the human services field who are far wiser and more knowledgeable than I in systems management.

Hopefully the human service system will have an impact on changing the attitude of society. I firmly believe that to the degree to which a society fulfills responsibility to persons who are developmentally disabled and their families, so much less will be the impact on parents. We will, therefore, find that having a child who is developmentally disabled may indeed be a life-shaking experience, but not necessarily a life-breaking one.

References

Dickman, I., with Dr. Sol Gordon (1985). *One miracle at a time.* New York, Simon and Shuster.

Featherstone, H. (1980). *A difference in the family: life with a disabled child.* New York, Basic Books, Inc.

Gold, M. (1972). Stimulus factors in skill training of retarded adolescents on a complex assembly tasks-acquisition, transfer and retention. *American Journal on Mental Deficiency, 76.*

Solnit, A.J., and Stark, M.N. (1961). Counseling the parents of the retarded. In A.A. Baumeister (Ed.), *Mental retardation: Appraisal, education and rehabilitation.* Chicago: Aldine Publishing Co.

CHAPTER VI

Transition: A Family Process

by Dorothy Kerzner Lipsky

transition, n.: passage from one state, stage, place or setting to another (*Oxford American Dictionary*).

As the deinstitutionalization movement continues to enable persons with developmental disabilities to return to the community, and as an estimated 250,000 to 300,000 students "age out" of the educational system annually, attention to transition issues related to education, work, and community opportunities is essential.

The definition of "transition" noted above suggests the variety of meanings of the word. In this chapter. we are concerned with its use in at least three aspects of the lives of persons with disabilities: in the transition from school to further education or work, from institution to community, and from family home to independent living. In effect, we are concerned with the passage from here to there.

For many persons with disabilitics not only the "here" but also the "there" is a place out of the mainstream, a setting which limits opportunities and inhibits capacity to grow, to contribute and give to others; and to be full-fledged members of society. This comes about due to aversion: prejudice, discrimination, an unaccommodating environment, the ways in which images about and attitudes toward persons with disabilities (and their families) become incorporated into public policies and human service programs, and the lack of knowledge and skills individuals with disabilities have been able to acquire.

While to a growing extent, albeit too slowly, there are analytic and programmatic efforts to address transition issues, professionals and parents have begun to realize that a free appropriate public education does not insure that young adults with handicapping conditions are provided automatically with vocational and employment opportunities. The following statistics illustrate our lack of success in preparing young people for work in the community:

- Qualification for employment is an implied promise of American education, but between 50 and 80 percent of working age adults who report a disability are jobless (U.S. Commission on Civil

Rights, 1983); these figures are confirmed by follow-up studies in Vermont, Virginia, and Colorado;

- Persons with disabilities who are employed earn substantially less than do able-bodied persons;
- Women and minorities with disabilities earn less than males and whites with disabilities (Edgar, Levine & Maddox, 1986);
- Persons with disabilities are 75 percent more likely to be employed part-time;
- Males with disabilities tend to be employed twice as much as females with disabilities, regardless of marital status (Hasazi, Gordon, & Roe, 1985);
- Standard fringe benefits (e.g., sick leave, vacation, insurance) generally are not available for persons with disabilities (Wehman, Kregecl, & Seyfarth, 1985).

Before turning our attention to the process of transition and its meaning for case management, it is essential to look at the societal context within which this process operates, for it is this societal context which defines, limits, and challenges these efforts. Goffman's (1963) provocative comment, "by definition, of course, we believe the person with a stigma is not quite human", is echoed by Ved Mehta (1985) "you see, we are confronted with a vast ignorance in the world about the handicapped, and they would not understand if we acted like normal people."

Increasingly, the earlier notions about disability are under attack. The traditional medical conceptualization is seen as limited and limiting and is being challenged by both a civil rights and environmental focus (Funk, 1987; Hahn, 1987). Indeed, the Congressionally-established and Presidentially-appointed National Council on the Handicapped (1986) endorses an environmental view, citing the Report of the United Nations Expert Group Meetings on Barrier-Free Design:

> Despite everything we can do, or hope to do, to assist each physically or mentally, disabled person achieve his or her maximum potential in life, our efforts will not succced until we have found the way to remove the obstacles to this goal directed by human society—the physical barriers we have created in public buildings, housing, transportation, houses of worship, centers of social life, and other community facilities—the social barriers we have evolved and accepted against those who vary more than a certain degree from what we have been conditioned to regard as normal. More people are forced into limited lives and made to suffer by these manmade obstacles than by any specific physical or mental disability (p. 7).

In this regard, the first national survey of persons with disabilities offers a number of important insights (Louis Harris & Associates, 1986).

- An overwhelming majority of all Americans with disabilities (74%) say they feel at least some sense of common identity with other people with disabilities. And, 45% feel the disabled are a minority group; this figure is over 50% for those 44 and younger.
- Nearly two-thirds of those of working age with disabilities do not work although 66% of this group want to work.
- Limits on individual's mobility and social activities are reported due to inadequate transportation by 49% and physical barriers to or in buildings by 40%.
- Overwhelming majorities favor public and private activities to enable disabled persons to join the workforce (95%) and to work better and communicate more easily with other workers (90%). Nearly as great a majority (78%) believe there should be less government spending for disabled persons who are able to work but do not.

This last set of attitudes is reflected in one of the major findings of the National Council on the Handicapped (1986). It states that, "Federal disability programs reflect an overemphasis on income support and an underemphasis on initiatives for equal opportunity, independence, and self-sufficiency" (p. 12).

The irrationality of the present programs was well expressed by Madeline Will (1985), Assistant Secretary, Office of Special Education and Rehabilitative Services, U.S. Department of Education:

Social Security was created to enhance the human dignity of workers, but as the Queen told Alice in Wonderland, "Words mean what I say they mean." In fiscal year 1983, the Social Security Administration spent 23 billion dollars in support payments that kept many disabled persons from working. Across the street, the Rehabilitation Services Administration spent one billion dollars to restore these same people to employment. And I note and underscore that's a twenty to one discrepancy. That is why I say the system itself may be more disabled than the clients it serves (p.79).

Leading journals and publications in the special education field are reflecting this change in perspective by publishing materials which challenges the current configuration of special education — separate, segregated, and second class (Algozzine & Maheady, 1985; Bickel & Bickel, 1986; Gartner & Lipsky, 1987; Stainback & Stainback, 1984). In reviewing Public Law 94-142 a decade after its passage, one of its key drafters (Walker, 1987) writes:

> The primary problem appears to be in our assumption about students and the consequences for the organizations of schools; that these are distinct groups of youngsters, disabled and non-disabled, and thus need distinct sets of services, special and general, which require divisions of funding, service delivery, and organizational patterns.

The consequence of these assumptions are seen in the denial to students with handicapping conditions of autonomy and choice-making, the characteristics of persons whom society respects. This failure is "not a function or the disability level of [the] children ... [but] an outcome of professional attitudes and practices..." (Guess, Benson, & Siegel-Causey, 1985, p. 84).

These same dysfunctional growth limiting characteristics affect services for adults. Assistant Secretary Will summarizes the areas requiring attention in her opening statement to a recent conference on transition:

> Programming for transition requires simultaneous attention to minimum wage issues, business incentives to offer employment, equal employment opportunity, and efforts to solve a structural unemployment situation.]t is also necessary to remove contingent barriers to independent living, transportation, and leisure time (Will, 1985, p. 82).

In summarizing the societal context within which the process takes place, we note major discrepancies. On the one hand, a limited and limiting physical and attitudinal environment exists, including the services for persons with disabilities, not simply in quality and quantity but in genesis and construct, in premises and assumptions, and in ideology. At the same time, there is a growing challenge from among the disabled themselves, from parents and other advocates, and from professionals. There is an assertion of the strength and wholeness of persons with disabilities: a claim to the uniqueness of their experience; a mobilizing of disabled people and their allies in stronger alliances to claim benefits as a matter of legal right, not charity; and challenges from both consumers and (some) providers as to the nature and quality of services.

Principles of Transition

The particulars of transition and six principles which must undergird that process are the subject of this section. These principles apply regardless of whether the transition is from school to educational or work options, or from institution to community setting, or from family home to independent living, In each case, these programs must be in the least restrictive environment for the individual. The principles are as follows:

1) Recognition that transition should be considered an integral part of the normal maturation and development process. Too often what is considered "normal" for the general population is viewed as exceptional when it concerns persons with disabilities. Just as the normal stresses and coping of parenthood often are ignored when considering the parents of children with disabilities (Lipsky, 1985a), so, too, there is a tendency when discussing "transition" to forget that it encompasses a process otherwise seen as normal.

2) Recognition that attention must be directed toward changing the environment to make it more accommodating.

3) Recognition that when addressing the individual with disabilities, one should start with strengths and capacities and build upon the potential of mutual support between and among persons with disabilities.

4) Recognition that the individual with disabilities is an integral part of a family system, and it can provide the context in which the individual lives, whose resources can be abetted and capacity and resilience increased in order to strengthen the individual.

5) Recognition that the goal of services is to build individual and family strength and capacity rather than to provide a lifetime of services.

6) Recognition that a solid foundation can be built which requires preparation and support in school, home, and employment setting, and includes adequate information, referral, advocacy, and social services to secure opportunities and services.

While transition is many things, it is not movement to a stable and fixed point. It is not the transition to a particular unchanging state, but rather a bridge to a range of opportunities: to live, to work, to participate, to contribute, in other words, to give to and to take from the society. As with the population in general, change over time is to be expected and encouraged; thus, "placement" in a job or living facility must not be considered the end, but the beginning of a lifelong process. The salience of this point is illustrated in a recent newspaper report. The story notes that increasingly "companies are taking on the more seriously retarded workers once thought unemployable in competitive jobs" (Ricklefs, 1986, page 35). Unfortunately, this encouraging news is balanced by the following comment of an Association for Retarded Citizens official discussing a man (IQ of 28) as a packer in a local supermarket, "Most people get bored in jobs like that, but David will be there forever..." (p. 35).

In a sense, the transition process from school to employment and adult life may be compared to those of a mountain climber — with successes and breakthroughs along with way. The difficult maneuvers require that work be done in preparation for the climb; that is, while the individual is still in school. There is the work at specific points along the path; that is, at the work site, college, or community residence. And along the path there is the process of the climb; the initial moves, the targets defined and refined, achievements noted, and new objectives set. Such is the transition process.

According to McDonnell, Wilcox, Boles, and Bellamy (n.d.):

> For all adolescents, transition is a time when the security of
> school is exchanged for more complex opportunities, risks, and
> services; when family roles and relationships are adjusted to
> acknowledge the graduates increased autonomy; and when the
> clear focus on learning as a personal and program objective is

normally replaced by the adult-oriented objective of independent performance, productivity, and community participation. (p. 1)

Research related to how adolescents in general make a transition and develop independence is pertinent here. Thus, for example, most young adults find jobs not as a result of being "placed," but through networks of family and acquaintances (Wegmann, Chapman, & Johnson, 1985); and, as they progress in the labor force, through work colleagues. Accordingly, we need to give attention to "transition strategies without formal services" (Bellamy, 1985, p. 11). This occurs, as Bellamy points out, through activities and opportunities for disabled persons to participate in family and friend-ship networks in the community and to be a part of the social networks which "normally" lead most people to jobs. In effect, the way to increase integration of disabled persons in the work force and the larger society in the future is to increase their participation and integration in the present.

This point is true also concerning community integration of the most severely impaired population. In describing the results of a program in a unit at the Syracuse Development Center (each person labelled as severely or profoundly retarded) who were taken on a week-long vacation to a popular resort, Baker and Salon (1986) note that rather than waiting for persons to demonstrate appropriate behavior in the institutional setting to show that they are "ready" for community opportunities, "integration itself is often the most effective way of addressing troublesome behavior..." (p. 178).

One must begin at the school level. While great progress has been made in the implementation of PL 94-142, research indicates that for many of the students presently served, their education remains segregated from the mainstream. As Walker (1987) points out, a decade after the implementation of the landmark law, the percentage of students with handicapping condi-tions who are educated in separate settings is no less than it was prior to the passage of the law. And even when "mainstreaming" takes place, often it is truncated, designed more to fit the school's administrative needs than the students' learning needs, and organized in such a way as almost to insure failure (Sansone and Zigmond, 1986).

Beyond these problems in the overall situation of special education, there are particulars concerning the provision of services preparatory to employment. Based on a national longitudinal study, Ownings and Stocking (1985) report:

- nearly twice as many handicapped as non-handicapped students, 22% versus 12%, drop out of high school; and
- fewer than a third of the handicapped students were enrolled in any vocational education programs.

Other studies note the absence of career-related objectives and transi-tional plans in IEPs (Cobb & Phelps, 1983); and "a lack of counselling and career planning services, parent involvement, comprehensive work experi-ence programs for youth while in school, and cooperative programming with vocational rehabilitation and other agencies..." (Chadsey-Rusch, Hanley-Maxwell, Phelps, & Rusch, 1986, p. 3)

Recently, activities designed to address these issues have been initiated. The Office of Special Education and Rehabilitative Services and the Administration on Developmental Disabilities have declared transition from student to adult status a national priority in their work. Transition has been a major priority of Madeleine Will (1984), and both the 1983 Amendments to the Education of The Handicapped Act (PL 98-199) and the Rehabilitation Act of 1973 (PL 93-112) have been sources of funds for model and demonstration projects (a total of 109 in FY 1984), and the Carl Perkins Act of 1984 makes vocational assessment a requirement under its equal access provisions.

There is an assumption that students in transition from school are leaving a somewhat organized provider system and entering a complex and confusing one which is not fully understood by service professionals, parents, and consumers. In point of fact, there are several hundreds of thousands of students leaving special education each year who require specialized services to obtain employment but have received an inadequate base for future learning of skills which employers are increasingly seeking. This failure in the education of students with handicapping conditions is especially harmful in the context of preparation for work. Not only does it provide an inadequate basis for future learning (Richards, 1981; Grain, 1984), it is directly detrimental when they present themselves for hiring. In addition to a quality basic education, students with handicapping conditions often require in-school preparation for the transition to work, programs of work experience, work skills preparation, opportunities for community-based work-site training, adequate occupational information, and job seeking skills. Given the importance that interpersonal skills play in employment, and the reality that integrated instruction contributes to improved social skills (Johnson, Rynders, Johnson, Schmidt, & Haiden, 1979), the limited extent to which students with handicapping conditions are integrated into school vocational programs (Eleventh Institute on Rehabilitative Issues, 1984) is a further impediment to their future success.

Much in the way of additional data could be presented to depict the lack or inadequacy of services in transition. For example, in 1976, as PL 94-142 was coming into effect, Stanfield (1976) reported that 94 percent of those leaving school (to a large degree the mildly handicapped), continued to live at home with their parents. He concluded, "graduation marked the beginning of a life of relative isolation from peers and segregation from the community" (p. 551). A follow-up study in 1983 in one of the nation's more progressive states unfortunately found little change (Brodsky, 1983). A recent national survey of post-school services for the severely disabled found not only few services available but also a lack of knowledge upon the part of state officials as to what was available (McDonnell, Wilcox, & Boles, 1986). This may in part be a reflection of the lack of priority being given to the topic.

Despite the social context in which issues of employment for persons with disabilities develop, a comprehensive study of programs that prepare individuals with disabilities for employment indicates that such programs focus solely on the remediation of deficits on the individual level (Lago-marcino & Rusch, 1987). What is needed prior to an individual focus is reevaluation at the organizational and systems level. Here one must address issues such as flexible work schedules, job sharing, job analysis and redesign, removal of architectural barriers and development of an accommodating physical environment. Only then is turning attention to individual deficits appropriate.

For example, transportation to work sites, training and educational locations, or recreation and leisure activities is a significant problem. Yet, the funding policies of various states often encourage schools and rehabilitation facilities to provide door-to-door bus service rather than to provide funds for travel training. Also, some programs continue to behave as if transportation other than to their doors is not their problem. The public policy issue of a transportation system inaccessible to those in such programs, however, means limits on the opportunities for the very persons the programs are designed to serve. Toward these ends, public policy changes, individual and group advocacy, and political action are appropriate tools (Handley-Maxwell, Rusch, & Rappaport, 1986).

Ecological Perspective

Just as persons with disabilities need to be seen in an environmental context, so, too, what is now being called ecological perspective (Chadsey-Rusch & Rusch, 1986) needs to he brought to the understanding of the workplace. The ecological perspective encompasses the physical, social, and organizational ecology. The physical ecology includes the architectural and physical design of the environment and job analysis of the particular requirements of the work. In the latter, if the goal is regular work, then the focus is on alternative ways of doing the work rather than on the individual's characteristics. The social ecology includes the social behaviors and social interaction patterns in the employment setting. Organizational ecology concerns the institutional context of the job; the type of management and supervisory patters, organization of the work place (overall size, size of units, etc.), salary, benefits, and opportunities for advancement.

In utilizing the ecological perspective in the work place, the key question relates to the appropriate intervention. One must address both the context and the individual, as well as the interplay between the two (Chadsey-Rusch & Rusch. 1986), rather than intervention strategies which focus "upon changing the individual with the handicap (Hanley-Maxwell, Rusch, & Rappaport, 1986). This is increasingly essential as reports indicate that individuals with disabilities are more likely to find failure in the work place as a result of deficits in social skills rather than job skills (Brickey, Browning, & Campbell, 1985; Greenspan & Shoultz, 1981; Hanley-Maxwell, Rusch, Chadsey-Rusch, & Renzaglia, 1986). Such deficits are also true for college graduates with disabilities according to a report which states that program participants have a "lack of socialization skills, sloppiness of dress, poor grooming, lack of appropriate table manners (Nathanson, Lambert, & Trachtenberg, 1986). Social networks are of particular importance in an ecological perspective. Such networks can reduce various types of occupational stress, improve certain health indicators, and improve adjustment to new situations (House, 198 I; Karan & Berger, 1986; O'Connor, 1983; Romer & Heller, 1983).

While we focused previously on examples in the work site, an ecological framework is an appropriate construct for a college setting as well. The norms and cultures of institutions vary — be they different units of a university (Katz & Rosenthal, 1986) or the same type of institution with different sponsorship, such as a community college (Apostoli, 1986). A college's sense of its mission affects both which students it admits and how they will be treated once admitted. The social networks at colleges involve fellow students, faculty, and administrators. To the extent that faculty are embedded in their disciplines and administrators in traditional rules and procedures, the introduction of persons with disabilities as students will be disruptive. As in the work place, therefore, an ecological approach requires attention to both the environment and the individual. What may be seen as a disabled student's deficit, requiring individual remediation, may be often overcome through an institutional change[1]. On the other hand, care needs to be taken to assure the quality of services are such that they actually benefit the individual. Thus, for example, while a learning disability may remain with an individual for life, skills taught and coping behaviors developed should be on series of levels so that at the post-graduate level it is no longer necessary to repeat the teaching of simple tasks such as training in time management (Katz & Rosenthal, 1986).

As we have indicated, most employment transition programs focus on remediation of the disabled individual's deficits rather than taking an environmental perspective; unfortunately, the same is true in transition programs which focus on community living. A multitude of areas for individual remediation have been delineated in the literature, e.g., personal hygiene, self-care skills, food management, social behavior, communications, home living skills, functional mathematics, recreation and leisure, community awareness and utilization (Rusch, Chadsey-Rusch, White & Gifford, 1985). However, too little policy attention has been given to environmental problems, such as the lack of availability of suitable housing (Lessard, 1982), accessible transportation (Bikson & Bikson, 1983; Clowers &

---

[1] Material developed by the Higher Education and the Handicapped Project of the American Council on Education, One Dupont Circle, Washington, D.C., offers valuable help for colleges in the development of reasonable accommodations. Among a myriad of directories, the most comprehensive is *Directory of College Facilities and Services for the Disabled* published by Oryx Press. Of course, depending upon the limits consequent upon the Supreme Court's decision in Grove City, colleges which receive federal funds are required by Section 504 of the Rehabilitation Act not to discriminate against otherwise qualified handicapped students and once admitted to make reasonable accommodations to make all programs available to them.

Belcher, 1979) or the broader question of autonomy. A review of the literature on independent living notes the absence of "any definitions of independent living at all" and comments that, "at times it may seem as though independent living skills are restricted to the clients' ability to take care of personal hygiene needs and make their own beds" (Harnisch, Chaplin, Fisher, & Tu, 1986, p. 58). These authors suggest that it may be more appropriate to "consider how the person uses, or the extent to which they are able to use, generic community services and whether they have the skills necessary for successful integration into the wider community" (p.59).

The high rate of recidivism among those who have been deinstitutionalized (Sutter, Mayeda, Yanagi, & Yee, 1980) and the social isolation of many persons (McDevitt, Smith, Schmidt, & Rosen, 1978; Schalback, Harper, & Carver, 1981; Bell, 1976) indicate the long way yet to go toward the achievement of real independent living. A place where individuals have functional independence and actual responsibility for the management of their own living arrangement (Lessard, 1982), enables people with disabilities to gain the physical and psychological benefits from having a real sense of control over their lives and the environments in which they live (Langer & Rodin, 1976).

This point is reinforced by a recent study comparing the views of directors of two types of living arrangements for individuals with developmental disabilities, between directors of the more restricted settings (lCF-MR group homes) and those of the less restricted settings (semi-supervised individual apartments and houses). There was a "cavernous gap" in the skills necessary to move from the more to the less restrictive setting, but the skills necessary to live in the less restrictive setting can be learned there (Rudrud & Vaudt, 1986). In other words, echoing the point made by Baker and Salon (1986), there is no logic to the notion of waiting for persons in institutional settings to show they are "ready" for less restrictive settings.

Transition Process

Up to this point, we have reviewed both parts of the transition process — first, at the school and then at the work site and community setting. While there are several stages to the transition process[2], we now will turn to a component of transition often mentioned but little attended to, namely, the contribution which parents and family members can make in that process.

Research related to strengths, coping patterns, and needs of families with members who have developmental disabilities is often deficient. At one level, there is the failure to develop systematic and theoretical bases for analysis including the contributions from various disciplines, and at another level there is the failure to see the individual as a member of a family

---

[2] For a thorough discussion of the transition process and its various stages, see the special issue, "Youth with Disability: The Transition Years" (1985).

(Turnbull, Brotherson, & Summers, 1985). Yet, according to theory, the family is the natural context for both growth and healing (Minuchin, 1981). Furthermore, the treatment of families as homogeneous and the failure to understand life cycle issues leads to a one-dimensional approach which focuses solely on the "problem". As such, it ignores both the family's capacity and the extent to which it shares experiences with all families (Lipsky, 1985a).

It is not that a family system with a member with a disability does not have stress of course, it does. Rather, the issue is in the management of and coping with the stress, and the resources provided to assist in that process (Lipsky, 1985a). Critical here is the need to recognize the heterogeneity among families, the variations of families' needs, and, within that reality, to provide resources during the transition process which incorporate flexibility. In doing this, the societal-provided resources build upon the families' strengths, providing supportive rather than substitutive assistance (Moroney, 1981).

This perspective — recognizing and building upon families' strengths — often is lacking in services and programs. Thus, for example, while many transition projects incorporate a parent training component, the training focus is on the professionals as trainer, instructor, and educator of parents. What is not recognized (nor expressed) is that professionals have much to learn from parents and that both must work together in a collaborative effort. The failure of professionals to see parents as partners in a collaborative effort is a missed opportunity for both to discover and understand the nature of the situation and the needs of the individuals. Based on a recent study of parent involvement in special education, a parent-professional partnership requires a full sharing of knowledge, skills, and experiences between the two sets of players (CSIE, 1984). Commitment to partnership rests on acceptance of the basic principle that the transitioning students will make better progress if their parents can work with professionals and if decision-making is a shared process. Since parents are different from professionals and their unique knowledge and commitment to a particular child is essential in the transition process, this special contribution must be given equal weight in assessment and decision-making.

Transition offers a unique set of opportunities for parents to be involved. Beyond their concerns for their child(ren), as noted above, there are a number of strengths parents have and can add to the transition process:

- Parents who are workers know about the world of employment and can offer insights about it to their own child(ren) and to others. If this is done in a systematic way, students can have the benefit of knowledge about jobs which goes beyond the experience of school and rehabilitation personnel.
- Parents as workers are part of a job network and can be resources in seeking jobs for their own child(ren) and those of others.
- Parents are sometimes employers and can hire workers with disabilities and encourage other employers to do so.

- Parents can be powerful advocates against discrimination and in seeking reasonable accommodations for their child(ren).
- Parents can join with each other and with the groups of persons with disabilities to exert pressure and gain changes in program, policies, and laws. Parents can reinforce school and rehabilitation efforts.
- Parents can provide emotional support for the student in the often stressful effort of decision-making, of presenting him/herself to prospective employers, facing judgement and (often) rejection. Parents can work with public institutions to identify needed services and establish new ones.

Parents' involvement is driven by more than their concern for their child's future. Parents are indirectly consumers of transition services. It is parents and family members who experience the painful results when transition efforts are unsuccessful. They must deal with discouragement when services are unavailable. Parents have a perspective on life planning that is difficult to match with episodic professional contact. Parents are in the best position to know the social support networks that will be available to assist a given individual over time. (McDonnell, Wilcox, Boles, & Bellamy, n.d., p. 8)

The issue is no longer whether to involve the family in the transition process but how. In doing this, a sensitive awareness must be maintained so that in concern for the family's needs, the needs of the individual with a disability are not ignored or diluted. To the extent that professionals may be more comfortable dealing with the nondisabled family members, the disabled individual's needs, indeed formulation of the issues, may not be addressed.

The essential characteristics of a transition process which incorporates the needs and strengths of the family and the individual with a disability who is a part of it may be viewed through a family support construct.[3] It applies equally well to the transition process and includes:

- ***EARLY INITIATION***— the system reaches out to the family at the beginning of the family's involvement;
- ***INTEGRATED SERVICES*** — while families will begin with one or another need, most often there will be a variety of needs, generally able to be met, by differing agencies. Whatever the institutional reasons for this, from the family's perspective, receipt of the array of needed services should not be a function of agency territorial lines, eligibility criteria, service plans, or professional prerogatives;
- ***UNIVERSAL ACCESS***— that is, wherever a family enters the system, all parts should be available to them;

---

[3] For an in-depth report on family support, see Agosta and Bradley (1985).

- *RECOGNITION OF A UNIQUE SET OF NEEDS*— while the totality of services may run a wide range for any individual family, it is its *unique set of needs* that must be addressed— in effect, selection from a *cafeteria of services;*
- *SUPPORT OF STRENGTHS*— while supports are designed to respond to needs, they should be designed to build on and bolster *strengths* and not focus on deficits;
- *SUPPORT GROUPS*— the shared experiences of families with a disabled member offer the basis for *mutual support* among such families;
- *RECOGNITION OF THE FAMILY'S CAPACITY* — paramount recognition needs to be given to the *family's capacity* including the ability to determine their own needs. Thus, in the determination of needs and the ways to meet them, the wishes of the family and of its members should be given priority (Lipsky, 1985b, p. 53).

The ideas here are congruent with McKnight's formulation of a community vision. He describes three overarching paradigms visions: 1) the therapeutic vision, which sees the well-being of individuals as growing from an environment composed of professionals, where there is a professional to meet every need; 2) the advocacy vision, which foresees a world in which belIed people will be in an environment protected by advocates and advocacy group in effect, a defensive wall of protection from a hostile community; and 3) the community vision. Here, "those who are labelled, exiled, treated, counseled, advised and protected are, instead, incorporated in the community where their contributions, capacities, gifts and fallibilities will allow a network of relationships, involving work, recreation, friendship, support and the political power of being a citizen."

Within this context there is a role for case management. In transition, 1) it is to understand the changes necessary in the ecological framework within the educational, rehabilitation, and employment systems; 2) to recognize the capacities of persons with disabilities and their families; 3) to provide information, referral, advocacy, and services as needed; and 4) to support them and their families.

References

Agosta, J. M., & Bradley, V. J. (Eds.) (1985). *Family care for persons with developmental disabilities: A growing commitment.* Boston, MA: Human Services Research Institute.

Algozzine, B., & Maheady, L. (1985), When all else fails, teach! *Exceptional Children, 52,* 487-488

Apostoli, B. D. (1986). Assimilating learning disabled young adults into the community environment. In New York Study Group on Transition.

Reflections on Transition: Model Programs for Youth with Disabilities. New York: Center for Advanced Study in Education, The Graduate School and University Center, University of New York.

Baker, M. J., & Salon, R. S. (1986). Setting free the captives: The power of community in liberating institutionalized adults from the bonds of the past. *Journal of the Association of Persons with Severe Handicaps, 11,* 3 176-18 I.

Bell, N. (1976). IQ as a factor in community lifestyle of previously institutionalized retardates. *Mental Retardation, 14,* 29-33.

Bellamy, G. T. (1985). Transition progress. *OSERS News in Print,1,* 1, 11.

Bickel, W., & Bickel, D. D. (1986). Effective schools, classrooms, and institutions: c_ Implications for special education. *Exceptional Children, 52,* 489-500.

Bikson, T. A., & Bikson, T. K. (1983). A five-year follow-up of sheltered workshop employees plied in competitive jobs. *Mental Retardation, 23,* 67-83.

Brodsky, M. (1983). Past high school experience of graduates with severe handicaps. Unpublished Ph.D. dissertation, University of Oregon, Eugene, OR

Bruininks, R., Hill, B., Lakin, C., & White, C. (1985). *Residential services for adults with developmental disabilities.* Logan, UT: Utah State University Developmental Center for Handicapped Persons.

Chadsey-Rusch, J., & Rusch, F. R. (1986). *The ecology of the workplace.* In J. Chadsey-Rusch, C. Hanley-Maxwell, L. A. Phelps and F. R. Rusch, *School-to-work transition issues and models.* Champaign, IL: Transition Institute, University of Illinois.

Clowers, M. R. & Belcher, S. A. (1979). A service delivery model for the severely disabled individual. *Rehabilitation Counseling Bulletin, 23,* 8-14.

Crain, R. L. (1984). *The quality of American high school graduates: What personnel officers say and do about it.* Washington, D.C.: National Institute of Education.

Edgar, E., Levine, P. & Maddox, M. (1985). *Washington State follow-up data of post-secondary special education students.* Seattle: University of Washington.

Eleventh Institute on Rehabilitation Issues. (1984). *Continuum of services' School to work.* Menomonie, Wisconsin: Research and Training Center, University of Wisconsin-Stout.

Funk, R. (1987). From caste to class. In A. Gartner and T. Joe (Eds.) *Images of the disabled / Disabling images.* New York: Praeger.

Gartner, A. Disabling help: Special education at the crossroads. *Exceptional Children, 53* (I), 72-76.

Gartner, A., & Joe, T. (Eds.). (1987). *Images of the disabled / disabling images.* New York: Praeger.

Gartner, A., & Lipsky, D. K. (1987). Capable of achievement and worthy of respect: Education for the handicapped as if they were full-fledged human beings. *Exceptional Children, 54*(l), 69-74.

Goffman, E. (1963). *Stigma: Notes on the management of spoiled identities.* Englewood Cliffs, New Jersey: Prentice-Hall.

Greenspan, S., & Shoultz, B. (1981). Why mentally retarded adults lose their jobs: Social competence as a factor in work adjustment. *Applied Research in Mental Retardation, 2* (1), 23-28.

Guess, D., Benson, M. A. & Siegel-Causey, E. (1985). Concepts and issues related to choice-making and autonomy among persons with severe disabilities. *Journal of The Association for Persons with Severe Handicaps, lO*, 79-86.

Hahn, H. (1 985). *The issues of employability: Economic perspectives of employment for disabled people.* New York: Work Rehabilitation Fund.

Hanley-Maxwell, C., Rusch, F. R., Chadsey-Rusch, J., & Renzagalia, A. (1986). Factors contributing to job terminations. In J. Chadsey-Rusch, C. Hanley-Maxwell, L. A. Phelps, and F. R. Rusch, (Eds.), *School-to-work transition issues and models.* Champaign, IL: Transition Institute, University of Illinois.

Harris, Louis, and Associates, Inc. (1986). *Disabled Americans' self-perceptions: Bringing disabled Americans into the mainstream.* New York: Louis Harris and Associates.

Hasazi, S. B., Gordon, L. R., & Roe, C. A. (1985). Factors associated with employment status of handicapped youth exiting high school for 1979-1983. *Exceptional Children, 51*, 455-469.

House, J. S. (1981). *Work stress and social support.* Reading, MA: Addison-Wesley Publishing Co.

Janicki, M. P., & Wisniewski, H. M. (Eds.). (1985). *Aging and developmental disabilities: Issues and approaches.* Baltimore, MD: Paul H. Brookes Publishing Co.

Johnson, R., Rynders, R., Johnson, D. W., Schmidt, B., & Haidu, S. (1979). Interaction between handicapped and non-handicapped teenagers as a function of situational goal structuring: Implications for mainstreaming. *American Educational Research Journal, 16*, 12, 161-167.

Karan, O. C., & Berger, C. (1986). Developing support networks for individuals who fail to achieve competitive employment. In F. R. Rusch, (Ed.), *Competitive employment issues and strategies.* Baltimore, MD: Paul H. Brookes Publishing Co.

Katz, B., & Rosenthal, I. (1986). Project CLASS: Career and learning assistance and support services. In New York Study Group on Transition. *Reflections on transition: Model programs for youth with disabilities.* New York: Center for Advanced Study in Education, The Graduate School and University Center, City University of New York.

Lagomarcino, T. R., & Rusch, F. R. (1987). Competitive employment: Overview and analysis of research focus. In V. B. Van Hassett, P. S. Strain, and M. Hersen, (Eds.), *Handbook of developmental and physical disabilities.* New York: Pergamon Press.

Langer, E. J. & Rodin, J. (1976). The effects of choice and enhanced personal responsibility for the aged. *Journal of Personality and Social Psychology, 34*, 191-198.

Lessard, K. J. (1982). *Developing community housing for the blind and deaf-blind students who have completed our training programs: What is our responsibility?* Vancouver, B.C: Association for Education of Visually Handicapped.

Lipsky, D. K. (1985a). A parental perspective on stress and coping. *American Journal of Orthopsychiatry, 55*, 614-617.

Lipsky, D. K. (1985b). *Family Supports in Rehabilitation in Israel.* New York: World Rehabilitation Fund.

McDevitt, S. C., Smith, P. M., Schmidt, D. W., & Rosen, M. (1978). The deinstitutionalized citizen: Adjustment and quality of life. *Mental Retardation, 16*, 22-24.

McDonnell, J. J., Wilcox, B. & Boles, S. M. (1986). Do we know enough to plan for transition? A national survey of state agencies responsible for services to persons with severe handicaps. *Journal of The Association for Persons with Severe Handicaps, 11*(1), 53-60.

McDonnell, J. J., Wilcox, B., Boles, S. M. & Bellamy, G. T. (n.d.). Issues in the transition from school to adult services: A survey of parents of secondary students with severe handicaps. Eugene: Center of Human Development, University of Oregon.

McKnight, J. L. (in press). Regenerating community. *Social Policy.*

Mehta, V. (1985). Personal history. *The New Yorker,* LXI, 39.

Minuchin, S. (1981). *Family Therapy Techniques.* Cambridge, MA: Harvard University Press.

Moroney, R. M. (1981). Public social policy: Impact on families with handicapped children. In J. L. Paul (Ed.), *Understanding and working with parents of children with special needs.* New York: Holt, Rinehart, and Winston.

Nathanson, R., Lambert, J., & Trachtenberg, L. (1986). Matching disabled college graduates with employers. In New York Study Group on Transition. *Reflections on Transition: Model Programs for Youths with Disabilities.* New York: Center for Advanced Study in Education, The Graduate School and University Center, City University of New York.

National Council on the Handicapped. (1986). *Toward Independence.* Washington, D.C.: U.S. Government Printing Office.

New York Study Group on Transition. (1986). *Reflections on transition: Model programs for youth with disabilities.* New York: Center for Advanced Study in Education, The Graduate School and University Center, City University of New York.

O'Connor, G. (1983). Social support of mentally retarded persons. *Mental Retardation, 21,* 187-196.

Owings, J., & Stocking, C. (1985). *High school and beyond: Characteristics of high school students who identify themselves as handicapped.* Washington, D.C.: National Center for Education Statistics.

Richards, E. L. (1981). Employer perceptions of the preparation of youth to work. Paper presented at the annual meeting of the American Education Research Association, Los Angeles, CA.

Ricklefs, R. (1986). Faced with shortages of skilled labor, employers hire more retarded workers. _Wall Street Journal_, (November 21).

Romer, D., & Heller, T. (1983). Social adaptation of mentally retarded adults in community settings: A social-ecological approach. _Applied Research in Mental Retardation, 4,_ 303-314.

Rudrud, E. H., & Vaudt, T. M. (1986). Prerequisite skills for semi-independent living services (SILS) placement. _Journal of the Association of Persons with Severe Handicaps, 11_(3), 176-181.

Rusch, F. R. (1986). Introduction to supported work. In G. Chadsey-Rusch, C. Hanley-Maxwell, L. A. Phelps, and F. R. Rusch (Eds.), _School-to-work transition issues and models._ Champaign, IL: Transition Institute, University of Illinois.

Sansone, J. & Zigmond, N. (1986). Evaluating mainstreaming through an analysis of students' schedules. _Exceptional Children, 52,_ 452-458.

Schalock, R., Harper, R. S., & Carver, G. (1981). Independent living placement: Five years later, _American Journal of Mental Deficiency, 86_(2) 70- 1 77.

Stainback, W., & Stainback, S. (1984). A rationale for the merger of special and regular education. _Exceptional Children, 51,_ 102-111.

Stanfield, J. S. (1976). Graduation: What happens to the retarded child when he grows up? In R. N. Anderson and J. G. Greer (Eds.), _Educating the severely and profoundly retarded._ Baltimore: University Park Press.

Turnbull, A. P., Brotherson, M. J., & Summers, J. A. (1985). The impact of deinstitutionalization on families: A family systems approach. In R. H. Bruininks and C. Lakin (Eds.), _Living and learning in the least restrictive environment._ Baltimore, MD: Paul H. Brookes Publishing Co.

Turnbull, H. R., & Turnbull, A. P. (1985). _Parents speak out: Then and now._ (2nd Ed.) Columbus, OH: Charles E. Merrill Publishing Co.

U. S. Commission on Civil Rights. (1983). _Accommodating the spectrum of disabilities._ Washington, D.C.: The Commission.

Vandergoot, D. (1985). The transition from school to work of youth with disabilities. Albertson, N.Y.: Employment Research and Training Center.

Walker, L. (1987). Procedural rights in the wrong system. In A. Gartner and T. Joe (Eds.), *Images of the disabled / Disabling images.* New York: Praeger.

Wegmann, R., Chapman, R., & Johnson, M. (1985). *Looking for work in the new economy.* Salt Lake City, UT: Olympus Publishing Co.

Will, M. (1984). *Bridges from school to working life.* Washington, D.C.: Office of Special Education and Rehabilitative Services, U.S. Department of Education.

Will, M. (1985). Opening remarks. *Journal of Adolescent Health Care, 6,* 79-83.

"Youth with Disability: The Transition Years." (1985). Special Issue, *Journal of Adolescent Health Care, 6*(2), 77-184.

CHAPTER VII

Local Issues in Case Management

by Lyle Wray (Dakota County, Minnesota)

Introduction

Service models directed toward persons with developmental disabilities have increasingly been centered on a number of core service themes. Some of these themes are: supplementing rather than supplanting existing helping networks, recognizing the paramount importance of flexibility in service delivery, individualization of the type, intensity, and timing of supports to families and individuals, choice from a service array, efforts to contain costs while providing an appropriate level of service, and the recognition of case management as a vital ingredient for supporting a dispersed, community-centered array of less restrictive service options.

These themes have been carried forward in the service system through small-scale community integration approaches which involve living and working arrangements which more closely resemble family scale situations. Consequently, a greater number and greater variety of service arrangements are being provided. Such arrangements require more thorough and complex case management systems. Some of the challenges being faced include the need to provide multiple services for many individuals—each service possibly being a choice from a menu of potential services—the need to respond to greater exposure to community demands and the need to provide for protection in a complex environment and to respond to a rapidly changing system.

The rapidly expanding, diverse, and multi-faceted community service system makes critical the effective operation of a system of coordination across various service elements provided to individuals, whether residential, employment, or other programs and services.

The pressure for community services and the rise of decentralization has had profound implications for local government's management of services. The return of responsibilities to states and localities under the "new federalism" over the past decade has involved decentralization. This, together with block funding arrangements and a withdrawl of the federal presence in some areas has spurred state and local efforts to better manage the overall service system.

The purpose of this chapter is to describe a number of issues related to providing effective case management at the local level, to attempt to interpret some of these issues, and to suggest an action agenda for future progress in responding to challenges at the local level.

Case Management Defined

In a few short years, the realization has grown that a minimal model of case management is not able to meet the challenges of responding to the needs of persons with developmental disabilities in concert with the themes described above. A more vigorous model is needed which involves more professional training and greater numbers of case managers if the services are to be developed, provided, and monitored at an acceptable level of quality.

Wray and Wieck (1985) reviewed a number of definitions of case management which varied widely in the scope of activities of case management, from a minimal brokerage model to an aggressive overall service management role. The more comprehensive concept of case management involved twelve components: outreach, client assessment, case planning, referral to service providers, advocacy for clients, direct casework, developing natural support systems, reassesment, advocacy for resource development, monitoring quality, public education, and crisis intervention. Recently, federal law provided an updated definition of *case management* in the Developmental Disabilities Assistance and Bill of Rights Act of 1987 (Public Law 100-146), Section 102 of which describes case management services:

> ... as activities to establish a potentially life-long, goal-
> oriented process for coordinating the range of assistance
> needed by persons with developmental disabilities and
> their families, which is designed to ensure accessibility,
> continuity of support and services and accountability and
> to ensure that the maximum potential of persons with
> developmental disabilities, productivity and integration
> into the community is attained.

Clearly, from this definition, much more is expected from the case management system than the minimal brokerage role definition of case management ofte seen today. Case management systems are increasingly being asked to respond to the need for improved individual service planning, the demand for greater program service development, the need to provide for tight monitoring of service delivery to individuals, the need to provide leadership for individual program planning, the need to provide a point of financial control and accountability for federal, state and local funds, and the need to effectively advocate for clients at the individual and program levels.

The United States General Accounting Office in 1988 issued a report on case management which reviewed a number of key themes in the area.

The case management system, then, must effectively address a number of critical components, each of which provide significant challenges for implementation at the local level. The approach in the remainder of the chapter is to identify barriers and possible solutions for challenges to effective case management operations so that systems may be improved.

Local Issues in Effective Case Management

For this paper, the results of several studies conducted on case management services for persons with developmental disabilities have been used to relate some of the barriers to effective case management and to suggest possible solutions. Two main studies have been drawn upon: the Minnesota Governor's Planning Council on Developmental Disabilities, *Policy Analysis Paper 24: Minnesota case management study: Executive Summary, A review of service coordination at Surrey Place Centre* (located in Toronto) (Wray & Wieck, 1986) and *Working together to meet the needs of North Dakotans with developmental disabilities* (Wray, Basuray, Miller, & Seiter, 1985).

Based on research in these studies and others, discussion is offered in the following areas: formal pre-service and in- service training for case managers, caseload size and case management resources, administrative burdens, service funding level and allocation, role conflicts faced by case managers, and effective management practices. In the concluding section, a number of positive steps are identified for improving case management services.

FORMAL PRE-SERVICE TRAINING FOR CASE MANAGERS

Although the critical nature of pre-service and inservice training is often acknowledged, the practice departs significantly from this value. It has been estimated that less than one percent of federal funds in the field of developmental disabilities are spent on training and research budgets. The field appears to be largely lacking in commitment to a human resources investment model in which staff are in essence the "productive equipment" for new initiatives to better serve persons with developmental disabilities. While corporations often devote between 2% and 10% of their expenditures to employee training and development, training expenditure levels in this field are generally inadequate. New initiatives frequently lack the substantial funds needed for training individuals and for changing the administrative system to support rapid innovation.

In addition to resource levels for training and development, it is well known the professional training often lags behind the requirements of the work place for a variety of reasons. The 1988 Minnesota study showed this to be true for case managers surveyed. In total, 80% of case managers reported no formal course work in case management and 61% reported no course work in developmental disabilities. In the case of supervisors, 97% indicated they had received no courses in developmental disabilities since becoming a case manager supervisor.

Another challenge comes from individual staff members who carry a number of different service responsibilities. In Minnesota over half the counties employed between one and two case managers. This has contributed to a so-called general case load model in which a case manager serves a number of client groups. Issues of scale pose a special challenge in smaller population areas, which often require staff to "wear many hats." Training is not usually provided to meet these multiple responsibilities. These staff need broader training in professional schools. Also, an in-service training model needs to be developed to respond to the special circumstances of the case manager with a general case load.

Professional training gaps can provide a major barrier to effective service in the system. There can be a two way gap in the pre-service training area: professional schools are not providing the kinds of skills needed by professionals in the field and professional schools may lack close awareness of the innovations evolving in day to day operations. The practice to research gap can cut both ways.

Curriculum design in professional schools should be a priority remedy for the long term in this area, with studies of front line staff competencies a sound foundation for curriculum restructuring based on the number of persons specializing in serving persons with special needs. The development of competency-based skill lists, for serving persons with special needs, should be a major part of the basis for professional education. Analysis of the skills as actually used by professionals in the field would be a useful tool to validate curriculum design. Some of the skill areas of high priority are: negotiation, knowledge of developmental disabilities, chairing meetings, problem solving, accountability, and recruiting community resources to address individual needs. Such competency lists would also be a useful foundation for in-service programs.

IN-SERVICE TRAINING

The field is evolving so rapidly that pre-service training of case managers cannot be adequate alone. There is a substantial burden to be placed on inservice training. In the 1988 Minnesota study, in contrast to the lack of formal pre- service training, 84% of supervisors reported inservice training in case management and developmental disabilities. As potential training topics, case managers listed: methods for negotiating with clients and service providers when there is a disagreement, methods for creative problem-solving and innovative thinking, how to develop an individual habilitation plan, methods for procuring accurate information related to service options, and how to assist clients to become their own case managers. Training is as yet relatively rare in areas such as applications for new technology in communications or robotics which might assist clients to remain more independent.

Inservice training should not be equated with attending conferences nor should it be confused with informational briefings on new laws or rules alone. Given the growing demands in the field, a more systematic plan of action is needed. Danley and Anthony (1982) pointed to several guidelines in developing training programs for case managers: (1) training should be tailored to the client outcome goals of an agency, (2) the goals of a training program should be measurable, observable, and capable of being evaluated, (3) selection of trainers should depend on clearly specifying the goals of the training and selecting trainers on behaviors relevant to those goals, and (4) the inability to retain good staff is in part a function of their being asked to achieve goals for which they do not have the needed training. Staff must understand what is expected of them and have the skills needed to perform their duties so that they are and feel competent to perform the tasks required of them.

Since skills are critically important, a thorough needs assessment of training needs for case managers, their supervisors and managers should be done. Based on this knowledge, responsive in-service training programs should be developed. In addition to systematic training needs assessments, steps such as systems of continuing education credit linked to employment and promotion, and convenient training delivery vehicles delivering skill building to case managers are some possible courses of action to strengthen skill development.

At a more basic level, the accessibility of training can be severely limited if case managers are not provided the opportunity to get away from their jobs to attend training. Often there are no substitute back-up programs so that some of the individual's duties will be assumed when they are away at training.

CASELOAD SIZE AND CASE MANAGEMENT RESOURCES

Another critical factor is the relatively small amount of resources provided to case managers to address significant responsiblities. This is often most clearly seen in the size of caseloads carried by case managers.

The 1988 Minnesota report found that the mean ratio of case manager to clients with developmental disabilities was 1:55. It might be worthy to note that Minnesota is in the top five states in the country in overall spending on human services programs. This ratio is found in a relatively resource rich environment. The 1988 Minnesota and the 1986 Ontario studies identified staff turnover and shortages as barriers to effective case management. In the 1985 North Dakota study, 69% of regional case managers reported case loads of greater than 50 persons. The ratios reported in the Minnesota and North Dakota studies are considerably higher, almost double, the ratios in states which have set ratios based upon resources needed to implement federal laws, and similar state laws and rules governing services to persons with developmental disabilities.

A proactive approach would involve detailed analysis of the staff time needed to attain the objectives of the operative laws, rules, and performance standards and to carry out rigorous priority setting activities with staff to streamline operations and to focus on the highest priority tasks.

It is very important to develop and disseminate models of case management task and case load analysis which can be used to make a case for appropriate resource levels at the local or state level. Showing how inadequate case management resources can lead to more costly service interventions which might otherwise have been prevented might also be a useful part of a resource strategy.

Given the dynamic nature of case management, it is becoming clear that low case loads are necessary to achieve the full potential of case management as a system. Personal leadership skills, great flexibility, and a vision of emerging service systems are increasingly demanded of case managers.

A prospect which needs to be faced at some point is what to do in the event that adequate case management resources are not provided. This is a complex question which is beyond the scope of this chapter. Some of the choices in response to such an eventuality include: empowering parents to act as case manager through a voucher and training system designed to reduce the administrative overhead of the service system, a conscious "triage" system where a set of criteria are developed to determine who gets case management services and for how long, a greater use of paraprofessionals to assume more and more of the duties of case managers at a lower cost, and investigation of non-traditional approaches to meeting the service coordination needs of clients. Federal funding of case management under the Medicaid program should be investigated to determine whether the benefits of such a move outweigh the disadvantages of limited client eligibility and regulatory overburden.

A debate on what to do in the absence of adequate resources may be healthy as an accompaniment to the review processes for allocating resources at the various levels of government. Additional research on case management is needed at a number of levels to evaluate current practice and future alternatives.

ADMINISTRATIVE BURDENS

Managing paper flow has become a very time consuming activity for case managers, rated the most serious barrier to effective case management by local case managers in the 1985 North Dakota, the 1986 Ontario, and the 1988 Minnesota studies. In the 1988 Minnesota study, a too large client case load size and the number of required meetings were rated as other major barriers. Minnesota supervisors also identified the amount of paperwork and case load size as major barriers.

A number of approaches might be taken to mitigate the paperwork burden. State and federal governments can examine record requirements to determine if there are methods of reducing the amount of paperwork required for case managers to compile. Studies may be made at the local or state level to analyze work flow to determine if more efficient means can be used to complete necessary paperwork.

Automation offers some hope in the "war on paper." A pilot laptop microcomputer project has been implemented in a number of Minnesota counties: Dakota, Itasca, Pine, Olmsted, St. Louis, and Chippewa (Dakota County, 1988). Case managers stored all critical client information on their personal computers. They have instant access to information on their entire case loads, along with the ability to update client information, prepare service plans and court documents, keep track of contacts and activities, and to take notes. The laptop computer enables a case manager to develop and complete a service plan at a client's team meeting or home. Individual needs and service plan objectives are entered on a form document stored in the laptop and the plan can be printed for signatures at the end of the meeting.

Further work needs to be done in looking at low cost options for entering data into a computer-based system. For example, optical scanning of forms can facilitate entering information with considerable savings of time. Also, greater use of case aides to process paper flow can free case managers for more client-centered work.

SERVICE FUNDING LEVEL AND ALLOCATION

Caires and Weil (1985) put the point succinctly: "The number one problem in the field of developmental disabilities, as well as in other human services fields, is money." It is appropriate to add that, to the extent that resources are available, they are often not deployed in the most effective manner but are rather allocated within restrictive service options such as state institutions.

In the 1985 North Dakota, the 1986 Ontario, and the 1988 Minnesota studies, insufficient funds and restrictions in the use of funds were also named as barriers, as was lack of program or other service options (Minnesota, 1988).

The issue of funding level and resource allocation is a major and complex one. If there are insufficient resources, it is not possible to meet the requirements of the definition of case management previously cited. The overall level of resources and their distribution across service strategies are therefore critical limiting factors to the overall system of case management.

Challenges to providing effective services through case management come both from the overall level of funding provided to the service system and from the way in which these funds are allocated to various services in the system. One can view the issue of resources as a challenge to effective case management as made up of several levels or layers. In the first layer lies the funding level and allocation for key service components which case managers may access to develop "service packages" for persons with developmental disabilities. In the second layer are the overall resources devoted to case management as a service which affect case load sizes and training, for examples. The role played by the case manager for client services is crucially linked to resources in these two layers.

At the system level, a number of funding issues come into play including resource allocation and financial disincentives for community living. The great majority of federal funding is lodged in the relatively restrictive Intermediate Care Facilities program with relatively meager resources devoted to family support or less restrictive, family scale living arrangements (see Braddock, Hemp, & Fujiara, 1986).

While the number of persons with developmental disabilities located in state institutions has dropped dramatically in the past fifteen years, the average daily costs of these facilities has dramatically risen as a result of such factors as higher standards of service and a lower census of individuals over which to spread administrative and operational overhead. A number of efforts have been made to remedy this situation through reform of the Medical Assistance system to provide funding preference to community living arrangements. The core nature of case management has been recognized in the recent versions of Medicaid reform in which case management is a mandatory service, providing a much needed structural change which should facilitate the continued development of community services for persons with developmental disabilities.

Another related issue is that there are major fiscal disincentives in some states for community placement, with community services costing local governments more than institutional services. There are a variety of ways in which this disincentive for community living is played out. There may be differing billing rates for community services than for state institutional services, with the latter costing local government less.

Financial steps can be taken to address the problem that the least restrictive environment is often the most expensive for the local units of government. For example, one measure could be to provide a funding arrangement in which true costs of services are billed to local government rather than having an artificially lower cost for institutions. Arrangements could be made to mitigate any sudden impacts of such a change by phasing in the system over a number of years.

With respect to the level and allocation of resources for services assembled by case managers, it is clear that case management is not a panacea. Case management alone cannot move a system if there is a significant resource shortage. By analogy, if the hotel system has no more capacity for providing rooms, a reservation system cannot solve that problem. While this is true, it is also true that even if there are more than enough resources but they are poorly organized, the job will not get done.

In many states in the country, there is substantial local discretion in raising and allocating funding to human services programs, including case management services. In the annual budget cycle, securing adequate resources for case management may be very difficult. Case management works by coordinating and managing individual services and as such may be less visible and defensible in budget setting processes than more direct "hard" services. Such competition betweeen direct and coordinative services at the local level suggests that federal or state policy may ultimately be needed to properly fully fund locally administered systems of case management. Future research is needed to document the case for improved quality and avoided costs as a result of more fully funded case management systems.

Another critical issue at the case management level is the degree of empowerment of the individual case managers and their supervisors in resource allocation in meeting individual needs. Austin (1981), in a General Accounting Office report, highlighted the resource allocation role of case managers. Case planning is a crucial resource allocation activity which has important implications for distribution of resources within a local delivery system. Properly designed and managed, a case management system should be close to the individual being served and be able to judge the types of services needed by a given individual. In addition, properly trained case managers with sufficient time can provide a crucial function in recruiting other community resources, whether on a formal or informal basis, to meet individual needs. Working with community groups to provide informal support systems, for example, requires time and skill to be applied.

Discretion over resource allocation and centralization of resource control are key case management design issues which need greater attention. Future research attention is merited in investigating case management models which expand the case manager's authority for resource allocation and increase flexiblity. In addition, insufficient funds or poorly allocated funds severely limit the effectiveness of the case manager to carry out their core responsibilities. Inadvertent financial penalties for developing community services should be addressed in concert with federal Medical Assistance reform for the Intermediate Care Facilties program. In developing these issues, a major consideration is providing the proper balance between underlying resource levels and allocation and the resources devoted to case management to provide maximum benefit to individuals being served.

ROLE CONFLICTS FACED BY CASE MANAGERS

Increasingly, the role of case manager is that of the *linchpin* of the system: performance or purchase of service contracting, service planning, supervision, evaluation, and service system change agents. This rather expansive role leaves open a number of conflicts in the roles held by case managers as well as conflicting perceptions among actors in the system on roles and performance. The 1986 Ontario and 1985 North Dakota studies, for example, found very different perceptions of the adequacy of performance in the case management system from the perspectives of parents and government case managers.

Case managers are at the meeting place of a number of critical forces surrounding clients in a service system: cost containment, individual protection, system change, and a constellation of other factors that bear on their daily work. As indicated by Weil and Karls (1985), case managers have multiple roles related to service provision and to accountability and cost effectiveness. In many cases, these roles involve conflicting duties—such as containing costs and advocating for clients. The substantial burdens of an expanded role for case managers then is compounded by inherent role conflicts.

Some of the role conflicts may be inherent to a "double agent" role of case managers representing the needs of individuals as well as the funding authorities. Research might address efforts to mitigate some of the role conflicts through various models such as having agencies independent of the funding authority play a role in resource decisions. The present knowledge level argues for research in the area to evaluate models involving differing configurations of agencies and individuals, and relationships to funding authority and individuals being served.

EFFECTIVE MANAGEMENT PRACTICES

The expansive definition of case management puts pressure on local managers to run a complex, highly accountable process of case management. Supervisory and financial controls as well as the development of more detailed procedures gain in importance with the greater complexity and size of the system. Supervisors are faced with ever more clients, more services, and often more complex service arrangements. The development of greater capacity to respond effectively to this pressure requires that a number of actions be taken in the areas of case load standards, quality assurance, and financial controls.

Some of the areas include the development of *case load and process standards* for case managers. Standards for how long it should take to develop an individual service plan, complete annual reviews, and negotiate service agreements are important basic components of such a system. Efforts to maintain *quality assurance* are also important since there is liability for the welfare of vulnerable and sometimes fragile persons in community settings.

There is a need for managers to address *financial controls* for services. Being more dispersed, with greater numbers of clients and funding arrangements, such a system poses challenges in cost control, much diminished since there were now relatively few large contracts for services which would directly involve case managers in the funding authorization loop. Such concepts as encumbrance accounting, and annualization of obligations are important in an evolving system and may be new to some case managers and to some agencies.

Informal ways of communicating with case managers may no longer suffice in complex systems service vulnerable people in community settings. In the 1985 North Dakota study, for example, there was a request for greater clarification of policy and procedures for carrying out the case management duties. Regretably, smaller operational units often do not have sufficient staff resources to develop detailed policy and procedural guidance for staff or to train them in carrying out policies and procedures once adopted. Responding to this challenge can be difficult for local managers with the press of many crises and little administrative support.

Improvement of management practices at the local level may be approached from a number of vantage points such as training, regulatory reform, and applications research. One of the important approaches is pre-service and inservice training in management and supervision issues. Strengthening management practices in areas such as supervision and coaching of employees can pay dividends if done within the overall framework of a skills development plan previously described.

A somewhat indirect approach to improving local management practices may be achieved by examining state and federal regulations with the goal of providing maximum flexibility for local managers. If federal and state regulations were to provide a greater relative focus upon results or outcomes for individuals in the regulatory system could afford a greater opportunity for local innovation and creativity in meeting individual needs. An overreliance on input based standards which hampers innovation and creativity.

The Road Ahead

Much remains to be done in facilitating effective case management systems to support the current and growing service demands of persons with special needs. It is clear that case management services are no panacea but work within an overall service system context. There is a shift of paradigms of service happening with a new generation of parents raised on mandatory integrated education and living arrangements for their children with developmental disabilities. Given resource limits, tough choices are likely on who gets served and how they get served. The question is how can case managers play an appropriate role in this emerging world. Some of the steps which might be taken include studies of case management, role clarification, and the applications of new technology.

Future work to improve case management can come from multi-state evaluations of case management led by the federal government. An identification of effective and ineffective practices and development of an agenda to facilitate community living for persons with developmental disabilities must occur on both the local and national levels.

There is great confusion among various professional disciplines such as medicine, social work, and providers over who is a case manager. The 1986 North Dakota study was directed in large part to a clarification of the roles of individuals acting to coordinate services within as opposed to across provider agencies. One mechanism identified in this cause was the interagency agreement. A clarification of roles for individuals working within and outside particular service providers may be appropriate at local and state government levels.

Empowering parents so that they will be less dependent upon the formal service system is worthy of exploration. In the nearer term, measures should be studied such as providing case managers with a flexible pool of funds to address individual needs in a flexible manner with guidance from parents.

Research is needed to show local managers how they may facilitate significant service system change at the local level in the context of tight resources. Demands for program and fiscal accountability call out for local innovations. Research carefully attuned to local realities can provide assistance in this venture.

Automation technology such as laptop computers may be used to stream-line the administrative burdens of case managers. Future technology may assist case managers and their supervisors in making decisions for individuals with developmental disabilities. The field of "expert systems" is one which may soon be applied in the field of services to persons with developmental disabilities (Hofmeister, 1986).

As the service system becomes more complex in an effort to provide more individualized, integrated services, additional research efforts must be addressed at efforts to assure that case management services rise to the challenge of providing the linch pin that holds the system together.

References

Austin, C. D. (1981) *Case management: Let us count the ways.* Paper presented at the Joint Meeting of the Scientific Gerontological Society and the Scientific and Educational Association on Gerontology, Toronto, Ontario, Canada,November 8-12.

Braddock, D., Hemp, R., Fujiara, G. (1986). *Public expenditures for mental retardation and developmental disabilities in the United States: State profiles* (Second edition). (Public Policy Monograph No. 29). Chicago: University of Illinois, Public Policy Analysis Program, Institute for Study of Developmental Disabilities.

Caires, K.B., & Weil, M. (1985). Developmentally disabled persons and their families. In M. Weil, & J.M. Karls (Eds.), *Case management in human service practice* (pp. 233-275). San Francisco: Jossey-Bass.

Danley, K., & Anthony, W. (1981). *The development of people power in CSP projects: Status, implications and future directions.* Boston: Boston University Rehabilitation and Research Training Center.

Dakota County Human Services (1988). *Microcomputer case management systems preliminary evaluation.* Saint Paul, MN: Developmental Disabilities Council, State Planning Agency.

Hofmeister, A.M., & Lubke, M.M. (1986). Expert systems: Implications for the diagnosis and treatment of learning   disabilities. *Learning Disabilities Quarterly, 9,* 133-137.

Minnesota University Affiliated Program. *Minnesota case management study: Executive summary* (Policy Analysis Series, Paper No. 24). Saint Paul, MN: Developmental Disabilities Council, State Planning Agency, February.

Public Law 100-146. The Developmental Disabilities Assistance and Bill of Rights Act of 1987.

United States General Accounting Office (1988). *Welfare reform: Bibliographies of case management and agency / client contracting.* Fact sheet for the Chairman, Committee on Governmental Affairs, United States Senate. (Document: GAO/HRD-88-61FS). Washington, DC: United States General Accounting Office.

Weil, M., & Karls, J.M. (1985). Historical origins and recent developments. In M. Weil & J.M. Karls (Eds.), *Case management in human service practice.* San Francisco: Jossey-Bass.

Wray, L.D., & Wieck, C.A. (1985). Moving persons with developmental disabilities toward less restrictive environments through case management. In K.C. Lakin & R.H. Bruininks (Eds.), *Strategies for achieving* Baltimore, MD: Paul H. Brookes Publishers.

Wray, L.D., & Wieck, C.A. (1986). *A review of service coordination at Surrey Place Centre.* Report to the Ontario Ministry of Community and Social Services. Toronto, Ontario, Canada.

ACKNOWLEDGMENT

Appreciation is extended to Colleen Wieck and Gay Bakken for their thoughtful comments on this manuscript.

CHAPTER VIII

Legal Perspectives of Case Management in Minnesota

by Luther A. Granquist

Since 1977, there has been a Minnesota Department of Public Welfare and, more recently, a Minnesota Department of Human Services rule governing provision of case management services by county social service agencies to persons with mental retardation. That rule was substantially amended in 1981 and 1984. The current rule, Minnesota Rules 9525.0015 to 9525.0165, was adopted in 1986. In its present form, it governs provision of case management services to persons with mental retardation and those persons who have a related condition.

Basic Provisions of Minnesota's Case Management Rule

The Minnesota rule has evolved into a rule which provides an excellent basis for provision of case management services. The rule incorporates standards for all the major components of the case management process:

DIAGNOSIS. The first step in the case management process is for the county agency to ensure that the person seeking services has a diagnosis as a person with mental retardation or a related condition (Minnesota Rules 9525.0045). Fundamentally, this step in the case management process is a determination of eligibility for case management services on the basis that the person has mental retardation or a related condition. The required diagnosis also includes a medical examination and preparation of a report on the social, physical, and environmental factors which may have contributed to the person's mental retardation.

ASSESSMENT. Assessments are required to determine the person's individual needs (Minnesota Rules 9525.0055). The assessment of individual service needs must address ten specified areas, but the assessment process must focus upon the person's skills or lack of skills which enable or prevent that person's full integration into community settings used by the general public. The rule defines "assessment" in terms which require an environmental or ecological assessment. The person's skills and behaviors are to be identified in conjunction with the "environmental, physical, medical, and health factors that affect development or remediation of the person's skills and behavior" (Minnesota Rules 9525.0015, subpart 2). The assessment process must consider the person's established support systems and must specifically address the physical and social environments which the person needs. The assessment process must result in specific service recommendations.

INDIVIDUAL SERVICE PLAN (ISP). The case manager designated by the county agency must develop an Individual Service Plan in conjunction with the individual, his/her guardian or conservator, and his/her advocate, if any. The ISP is the overall planning document developed by the county agency. It must include a summary of diagnostic and assessment information which leads to identification of the type, amount, and frequency of all service needs. The ISP must establish long range and annual goals for the person and state the actions which will be taken by the county agency to develop or to obtain needed services.

AUTHORIZATION OF SERVICES. The case manager from the county agency may only authorize services if a determination has been made that the proposed provider is able to provide the service(s) in accordance with the Individual Service Plan. This provider competency determination is the key case management responsibility. The county agency must enter into a contract with the service provider which includes an explicit description of the services to be provided.

INDIVIDUAL HABILITATION PLAN (IHP). The case manager must develop an Individual Habilitation Plan in conjunction with an interdisciplinary team including those persons involved in the development of the ISP as well as representatives of service providers. This IHP must integrate the services of all providers and must be designed to achieve the outcomes specified in the ISP (Minnesota Rules 9525.0105).

MONITORING AND QUALITY ASSURANCE. The rule specifies a process which the case manager must follow in monitoring provision of service (Minnesota Rules 9525.01 IS) and the standards by which the adequacy of service is to be judged (Minnesota Rules 9525.0125). The process requires reviewing records, observing implementation of the ISP and IHP, and visiting with the person receiving services. The basic substantive standard is whether services are being provided in accordance with the ISP and IHP, but the case manager must also consider whether active treatment and habilitation services are being provided, whether the legal rights of the person are being protected, and whether that person and any guardian or conservator are satisfied with the services provided.

SERVICE DEVELOPMENT NEED DETERMINATION. The rule also requires the county agency to undertake a general planning process leading to development of new services or modification of existing services within the county (Minnesota Rules 9525.0145). This process is dependent upon identification of individual service needs in the ISP.

The purpose of the rule is that the steps in the case management process must be undertaken "so that the services meet the level of the person's need in the least restrictive environment and in a cost-effective manner" (Minnesota Rules 9525.0025, subpart 2). The rule defines "least restrictive environment" in terms which include qualitative indicia of services such as promoting the independence of the persons, limiting supervision and physical control over the individual, increasing interactions between the person and those in the general public who do not have disabilities, implementing daily, monthly, and annual schedules which closely approximate those of the general public, and using materials and methods of instruction which are appropriate for the person's chronological age and adapted to individual need.

The rule requires cost-effective services. The rule emphasizes both the effectiveness of the service and cost containment. Only services which are necessary to meet individual needs are to be provided. To be effective, those services must, in fact, meet the person's needs.

The key question for the person receiving case management services is whether the case management process will lead to provision of services which actually do meet the individual's needs in the least restrictive environment and in a cost-effective manner. If the process is implemented in accordance with the standards in the rule, that outcome should be achieved. More often than not, however, the process is, not implemented to that end. The key legal issue, therefore, is whether appropriate and necessary action will be taken to ensure that the standards in the rule are enforced.

State Enforcement of Case Management Rule

Minnesota has established a system in which community social services, including case management services and other services to persons with mental retardation or a related condition, are administered by county agencies under the supervision of the Commissioner of Human Services (Minnesota Statutes 256E.02). This case management process is authorized by Minnesota Statutes 256B.092. The Commissioner was directed by the legislature to promulgate a case management rule which sets standards for case management and which the county agency is to implement in a flexible and individualized manner (Minnesota Statutes 256B.503).

The rule includes a provision which allows the Commissioner to issue written orders to county agencies in circumstances in which a county agency has failed to comply with the standards in the case management rule. A process for a county agency to request reconsideration by the Commissioner of this order is established. The Commissioner's decision on reconsideration is final unless legal action is taken in the state district court (Minnesota Rules 9525.0165). To date, this enforcement process has never been implemented by the Commissioner of Human Services.

The Commissioner is also authorized by statute to certify a reduction of up to 20% of the county's annual funding under the Community Social Services Act if a county agency is not in compliance with an applicable department rule (Minnesota Statutes 256E.08, subd. 1). The county agency may expand any funding reduction imposed. The Commissioner of Human Services has never taken the statutorily authorized action of reducing county funding.

The Commissioner's failure to act, however, is not a result of total compliance with provisions of the case management rule by county agencies. The Commissioner has undertaken reviews of case management services provided to individuals throughout the state and determined that there are many areas in which case management services do not comply with the case management rule. Whatever the reasons may be for the Commissioner's failure to exercise the authority granted by statute and rule, persons with mental retardation or a related condition cannot depend upon the Commissioner independently to take the action necessary to ensure compliance with the rule.

Individual Enforcement of Case Management Responsibilities

For many years, Minnesota has employed an administrative review process by which persons receiving public benefits or social services from county agencies may seek review of county agency determinations before a referee appointed by the Commissioner of Human Services. This "welfare fair hearing process" has been used in circumstances in which county agencies find an individual ineligible for services or a county agency fails to provide case management services with reasonable promptness. The statutory language focuses, however, upon denial, suspension, reduction, or termination of services, or failure to act with reasonable promptness (Minnesota Statute 256.045, subd. 3[a]). The Commissioner's authority to decide issues involving the quality of case management services or the quality of services provided the individual was in doubt, for the individual's claim would have to fit within statutory language developed and applied primarily in appeals involving monetary public benefits.

In 1987, the Minnesota legislature, as a condition to settlement of a lawsuit in the federal district court involving persons who are or have been residents of the state institutions, added a section to the welfare fair hearing statute which provides for "case management appeals" (Minnesota Statutes 256.045, subd. 4a). Persons who were dissatisfied with the quality of case management services provided were authorized by this new legislation to request a conciliation conference with the county agency. At this conference a representative of the Department of Human Services would seek to assist the person with mental retardation and the county agency to reach a resolution of the dispute without the need for a hearing. This conciliation process was modeled upon, but is not identical to, the conciliation conference process available to persons receiving special education services in the public schools.

If the results of the conciliation conference are not satisfactory, the person receiving case management services may request a hearing before a referee appointed by the Commissioner. Two types of issues may be presented on such appeals:

- whether case management services have been provided in accordance with applicable laws and rules; and
- whether the county agency assured that the services identified in the person's ISP have been delivered in accordance with the laws and rules governing the provision of those services.

This appeal process provides clear authorization for the person to seek review of the quality of case management services and the quality of the services actually arranged by the county agency.

The Conciliation Conference Process

The Conciliation Conference Process is intended to be an informal process which can be used by the person with mental retardation or his/her parent or guardian without legal representation. The process is initiated by a letter to the county agency which only needs to state that a conciliation conference is requested. The Commissioner's representative has the responsibility to see that issues are identified at the conference and that an effort is made to resolve them. The county agency must prepare a report after the conference stating what action the county agency is going to take and when that action will occur.

If the issues are relatively narrow and focus on specific actions which the county agency has not taken, the conciliation conference process can work effectively to prompt the county agency, for example, to undertake a specific assessment or develop an ISP. If however, the issues involve the bit of the assessment, of the ISP, or of the services arranged for the person by the county agency, it is far more difficult to resolve the issues without assistance from advocates familiar with the requirements of the rule and with program standards.

Inadequate provision of services frequently is the result of inadequate implementation of the case management process. When individual needs have not been assessed thoroughly and appropriately, ISPs and IHPs are developed which do not specify the services required. The "Action Plan" needed in a conciliation conference when pervasive deficiencies in both service delivery and case management are at issue will be detailed. The conciliation conference process works best in those circumstances when the advocate prepares a detailed Action Plan prior to the conciliation conference. The Action Plan should be given to the county agency with the request for a conciliation conference as soon as possible thereafter. If an Action Plan is not proposed until the conciliation conference, county agency personnel may say they need study it, making it difficult to reach any definitive agreements at the conference itself. County agency personnel frequently lack both an understanding of the requirements of the rule and the program expertise necessary to respond to an Action Plan. In such cases, where county personnel are uninformed, the discussion of an Action Plan may be more an educational exercise for the benefit of county agency personnel than an informed discussion of the steps which are needed to ensure that appropriate services are developed and implemented.

Nevertheless, the conciliation conference process is a beneficial one. It allows advocates for persons with mental retardation to identify, in detail, the actions which the county agency should take. If the county agency is committed to provision of service, the ultimate result is likely to be an improvement in service delivery, but never, it seems, in accordance with the schedule incorporated in the Action Plan. In some instances, the threat of a subsequent appeal hearing has prompted county agencies to take some of the actions which should be taken.

The Appeal Hearing

Persons receiving case management services have up to 90 days after the conciliation conference to request a hearing before a referee appointed by the Commissioner of Human Services. This 90-day period was written into the law to provide the county agencies an opportunity to fulfill the agreements reached at the conciliation conference. Should no agreement or an inadequate agreement be reached, the appeals process can start as soon as the conciliation conference is completed. The appeal may be initiated by an informal letter to the county agency or to the Commissioner. A formal Notice of Appeal may also be submitted, which can be very general or quite specific. The Commissioner has ruled that the person bringing the appeal is not limited on appeal solely to those issues raised at the conciliation conference. It is certainly better practice to raise all of the relevant issues at the conciliation conference and to incorporate a specific statement of the issues for the appeal in the letter or notice which triggers that appeal.

Although not specified in the statute, the Appeals Referees have issued pre-hearing orders which specify such things as sharing of witness lists, development of exhibits, and provision for the county agency to produce appropriate records. The Appeals Referees also have the power to issue subpoenas.

While there is no requirement for representation by either party to the appeal by an attorney, representation by an experienced advocate or by an attorney is very helpful to the person with developmental disabilities. Unlike many other welfare "fair hearings," case management appeals tend to last a minimum of a day or two because the issues are quite broad and, generally, there is substantial documentary evidence to be considered. All evidence, except that privileged by law, which is "commonly accepted by reasonable people in the conduct of their affairs as having probative value with respect to the issue" will be received (Minnesota Statutes 256.045, subdivision 4). There is a structured informal it)' to these hearings, which are even more informal if attorneys are not involved.

After the hearing and after receipt of any memoranda that are submitted by the parties, the referee makes recommended findings, conclusions of law, and a recommended order for review by the Commissioner or by the Commissioner's delegate. The statute authorizes the Commissioner to direct the county agencies "to take those actions necessary to comply with applicable laws or rules" (Minnesota Statutes 256.045, subdivision 4a). The Commissioner also has the power to exercise discretion in framing relief: "In all matters dealing with human services committed by law to the discretion of the local agency, the Commissioner's judgment may be substituted for that of the local agency" (Minnesota Statute 256.045, subdivision 6).

Either the county agency or the person bringing the appeal may seek judicial review in the state district court.

Effectiveness of the Appeal Process

In the limited number of appeals taken since the legislature authorized case management appeals, the Commissioner has demonstrated some willingness to issue orders which state in detailed terms the actions which the county agency must take to fulfill the various steps in the appeal process. A reviewing court upheld a detailed order with respect to assessment actions by noting that the "drafters of the rule contemplated an assessment process which responds to variables unique to the handicapped person rather than a generic assessment process." The court noted the unique needs of this individual and concluded the Commissioner's order properly tailored the assessment process to those unique needs.

Specific orders detailing the action to be taken are necessary, for the standards in the case management rule are just that, standards, not a detailed blueprint specifying how case management activity must be undertaken in each case. No rule could include all of the detailed specifications applicable to a particular person.

The Commissioner's orders, however, tend to focus on one step or another in the case management process without viewing the case management process as a whole. In this respect, the Commissioner mirrors the actions of county agencies. County agencies tend to focus upon the discrete steps in the case management process without consideration of the purpose which case management is to serve—provision of services which meet individual needs in the least restrictive environment and in a cost-effective manner. The appeal process will work effectively only when the Commissioner analyzes the standards for each step in the case management process in light of the outcome required to be achieved by that process. For instance, the requirement for assessments must be viewed in terms of what information about the individual needs to be obtained in order to develop an ISP which will identify the type, amount, and frequency of all needed services as is required by the rule. Furthermore, the assessment process is a building block for the development of short-term objectives in the IHP.

The Commissioner has recognized, although not explicitly, the relationship between identification of the type, amount, and frequency of service needs in the ISP and the service authorization process by providing that the ISP must identify the competency required to deliver the needed service so that the case manager can make the service authorization determination required—that the provider is *able* to deliver services in accordance with the ISP. However, the Commissioner has not, in decisions issued, articulated the analytic framework that is essential for thoughtful implementation of the case management process.

Any attorney who has been involved with legal actions, whether in federal or state court or before administrative agencies, soon learns that detailed orders specifying action to be taken by government personnel are not self-enforcing. One problem is, in part, the lack of case managers with the prerequisite training and expertise to do the job. A second problem is the size of the case manager's caseload. A third problem is, in some instances, the lack of administrative support within the county agency for a case manager who seeks to do the job right. The Minnesota appeals process leads to an order by the Commissioner, but the person bringing the appeal has no ready remedy against an agency which does not comply. (The failure of the Department of Human Services to exercise its enforcement powers has already been noted.) Court action is necessary to enforce the Commissioner's order. In the meantime, the county agency has little to lose by failing to comply with the order.

Challenging Professional Judgment

If a county agency has failed to do particular assessments, to write an ISP, or to develop an IHP, a case management appeal order which requires that the assessment be done, or that an ISP or IHP be completed, will not be likely to threaten county agency or provider personnel. The rule clearly requires this action. The fact that the necessary action has not been taken cannot be disputed. The responsible case manager may be chagrined that required steps in the case management process were not completed, but the reasons for failing to do so may be perceived as impersonal factors such as caseload size and other time commitments.

This situation is different when the issue is the quality of assessments, ISPs or IHPs. The situation is also different when fundamental issues regarding quality of services provided are raised. In those circumstances, the professional performance of case managers and provider personnel is directly at issue. Their work product and performance are scrutinized and challenged. This scrutiny heightens tension and can cause animosity in the adjudicative process.

The Minnesota statute requires analysis of professional performance in the appeal process. Whether case management services have been provided "in accordance with applicable laws or rules" or whether services "have been delivered in accordance with the laws and rules governing the provision of those services" (Minnesota Statutes 256.045, subd. 4a) can only be determined by comparing action taken by the responsible professional personnel with regulatory and statutory standards. In this respect, adjudication of these issues under the Minnesota appeals statute differ from challenges to professional judgment in a constitutional context.

The United States Supreme Court, in *Youngberg v. Romeo*, ruled that deference must be given to professional judgment by courts deciding constitutional issues. Courts are required, in that context, to consider decisions by professionals as presumptively valid unless the decision was "such a substantial departure from accepted professional judgment, practice or standards as to demonstrate that the person responsible actually did not base the decision on such a judgment" *Youngberg v. Romeo*, 457 U.S. 307, 323 (1982). This standard differs, however, from a standard which requires professional decisions, whether by case managers or by providers, to be scrutinized in terms of compliance with regulatory requirements.

It is crucial that persons with developmental disabilities have a forum in which issues about quality of service can be posed and decided. When service needs are not met in the least restrictive environment and in a cost-effective manner as required by the Minnesota case management rule, the person entitled to those services must be able to challenge the professional decisions made (or not made) which have led to inadequate service delivery. The Department of Human Services, as the administrative agency responsible for promulgation and enforcement of the rule, is the appropriate agency to establish an appeal mechanism to resolve these issues of professional performance. There will, however, be some professional blood shed along the way.

A real issue is whether the challenge to professional judgment in the appeals process will make it more difficult to achieve the changes in service delivery necessary for the desired outcome to be realized. Case managers and service providers react differently when challenged in this way. Some strive to do a better job. Some become immobilized. Others simply quit. Accountability through an adjudicative process can create new problems.

As a tactical matter, the advocate or attorney must be professional in the hearing process. Thorough investigation and research are essential. There is no excuse for lack of preparation. There is also no excuse for any lack of civility in the hearing process. The fact remains, however, that to prove lack of quality services often requires proof of professional incompetence.

The relief sought in the hearing process must, therefore, address this root cause of inadequate service. An order which directs a case manager to perform tasks which the case manager does not know how to perform will not ensure that needed services will be provided. Similarly, an order that requires the county agency to arrange for services which meet individual needs is fruitless if service provider personnel lack the skills to provide needed services.

The Minnesota appeals statute provides that the Commissioner may order county agencies to take those actions necessary to comply with applicable laws and rules. A major issue, not yet decided, is whether the Commissioner will determine in the appeal process that it is necessary to require county agencies to provide needed training and technical assistance to case managers. A related issue is whether the appeal process can be used to require county agencies, in the service authorization and contracting process, to identify deficiencies in performance by the service provider and to require the technical assistance and training the provider and the provider's staff need to accomplish the job. The legal framework to impose these requirements is present within the rule. As a practical matter, the desired service outcomes will not be achieved unless technical assistance and training are required for both case managers and service providers.

In theory, there are probably better and less painful ways to achieve the change which is necessary in the quality of service provided to persons with mental retardation. County and state agencies which are committed to provision of quality services should develop internal quality control procedures which will lead to changes in the quality of services without the need for prompting through an adversarial process. That day has not yet dawned in Minnesota. A forum for challenging the quality of service on an individual, case-by-case basis is an essential part of a quality assurance system, for it allows systemic issues with regard to case manager and provider performance to be addressed in a context which focuses on the crucial issue—meeting that individual's needs in the least restrictive environment.

CHAPTER IX

P.L. 99-457 - Challenges and Changes for Early Intervention

Carla Peterson - University of Minnesota[1]

Early intervention services for children with special needs and their families have been widely established in the latter half of the 1980's. These efforts were prompted primarily by passage of the Education of the Handicapped Amendments (P.L. 99-457) in 1986, which represents the *first national* policy to provide services to very young children with disabilities.

Providing appropriate services to infants and toddlers has proven to be a challenging task. By definition, this population is unique in many respects and tailoring services to reflect this has been necessary. Tasks undertaken to guide the development of early intervention efforts have built upon previous work in several fields, have required levels of interdisciplinary cooperation previously unused, and have caused professionals to rethink approaches to service delivery.

Public Law 99-457 holds major implications for policy development and implementation, provision of interventions, and strategies for delivering services. This chapter discusses these implications and some historical factors which led to its adoption as national policy. A major focus of the chapter will be on the Individualized Family Service Plan (IFSP) because this will illustrate the many practical considerations needing examination.

HISTORICAL PERSPECTIVES ON THE PASSAGE OF P.L. 99-457

Services to infants and young children with special needs have been provided for some years by a variety of agencies in a myriad of ways. However, services to young children and their families have not been universally available and there has been little consistency in either philosophy or approach from program to program or area to area (White & Casto, 1989).

At least three different purposes for providing intervention for infants with developmental disabilities and their families, each stemming from

[1] *Preparation of this manuscript was supported by U. S. Department of Education Grant N. Goo8730527-89, to Vanderbilt University and the University of Minnesota and by Administration on Developmental Disabilities Grant No. 07- D0282 to the University of Minnesota.*

different underlying rationale, continue to be identified today (Odom, Yoder, & Hill, 1988). One identified purpose is prevention of eventual developmental delays if services are initiated soon after birth. A second purpose is to directly effect changes in the infant's development, behavioral repertoire, or relationships with caregivers in the belief that these will prove beneficial to the infant's overall developmental course. Lastly, some programs are designed to positively affect the infant through systemic change within the family.

Today, early intervention programs are most often designed to address the needs of young children and their family members from the perspective of the third purpose. The move toward this "family systems perspective" has roots within at least three important movements in American society, specifically, to improve and expand services for persons with disabilities, to fully integrate persons with disabilities and to expand parental involvement in their children's education.

Earliest services for young children with disabilities were designed to rehabilitate functional and cognitive skills deficits. Until the latter half of the 1960's, service delivery systems were focused on direct intervention with children. Only later was the interaction between child and caregiver clearly acknowledged as an important force in a child's development. However, there were no real guidelines or models for use with very young children and professionals were forced to rely on techniques that had been developed for use with older children and adapted for use with infants and toddlers (Smith, 1988).

Prior to the 1950's, attitudes toward both persons with handicaps and their parents were largely negative. Beginning in that same decade, a movement toward a more humanitarian and optimistic view of disability gained momentum, largely due to efforts of parents joining forces to demand improved services for their children (Benson & Turnbull, 1986).

During the 1960's, the strong influence on a child's development played by family circumstances, as well as the importance of early development on long term outcome, drew attention and fueled debate in the scientific community (Hunt, 1961; Bloom, 1964; Bronfenbrenner, 1974). Concurrently, pressure to provide compensatory education for economically disadvantaged children began to be applied in the judicial and legislative arenas (Turnbull & Winton, 1984). Ultimately public policy and practice were affected, resulting in the authorization of Project Head Start, especially significant as it incorporated the first requirements for parental involvement.

The perceived need for parental involvement in early childhood programs was argued from many different perspectives, however. Some reflected a deficit model, in which parents were viewed as lacking essential child-rearing knowledge and skills (Foster, Berger & McLean, 1981) or as having politically based deficits (Valentine & Stark, 1979). Some represented the belief that intervention with parents would benefit not only the target child, but also other children in the home (Gray, 1971; Goodson &

Hess, 1975). Some viewed parents as consumers of and potential advocates for early childhood programs (Lillie, 1975) and as such having the right to involvement and assurance that services were consistent with their own values (Yawkey & Bakawa-Evanson, 1975). Still others saw parental involvement as important for consistency and as an aid in the transfer of learning across environments (Lillie, 1975; Hayden, 1976).

Research findings on human attachment behavior provide additional support for parental involvement. Longitudinal studies have highlighted that long term, negative consequences in social, intellectual, and affective development are often associated with poor quality attachment relationships between infants and their mothers (Erickson, Sroufe & Egeland, 1985). Also, infants with handicaps have been shown to be deficient in the behaviors that facilitate both interaction with mothers and secure attachment (Ramey, Bell & Gowen, 1980).

The passage of P.L. 94-142, the most significant landmark event shaping parental roles, was both a culmination and reflection of prior events and perspectives (Benson & Turnbull, 1986). The primary role expected of parents was that of educational decision-maker. It established guidelines for educational agencies regarding parental notification, consent, and decision making which, in actuality, provided parents with the authority to protect their children's rights. The secondary role set forth for parents was that of intervenor.

In passing P.L. 91-142, Congress made two assumptions regarding parental involvement. The first was that it would increase the assurance of students' rights, and the second is that the educational process would extend into the home, thereby increasing the continuity and effectiveness of educational programs. The students, however, continued to be seen as the beneficiaries and foci of these efforts (Benson & Turnbull, 1986).

In 1986, the United States Congress passed Public Law 99-457, the Education of the Handicapped Act Amendments. This important addition to P.L. 94-142 has called for an expansion of parents' roles in both decision making and intervention activities, with parents viewed as part of the intervention team. In addition to this, the very notion of early intervention has been expanded from primarily a child-centered focus to a concentration on children and their family members. Parents and/or other family members may now themselves be the targets or recipients of interventions and services. This law calls for identification of eligible children below the age of three, and the expansion of services beyond those of education. Instead, many different educational, health, and social service agencies are charged with working cooperatively to develop and implement an effective and efficient plan to address the needs of each family member individually and the family unit as a whole.

IMPLICATIONS OF P.L. 99-457

Representing the first national policy to provide services to very young children with disabilities, the provisions of P.L. 99-457 depart from previous policies in two major ways. Namely, they are family-centered in nature, and they emphasize interagency collaboration (Smith, 1988). Under P.L. 99-457, services are aimed at an entire family rather than focused on only the child with special needs, thus acknowledging the long-term benefits support can offer to both the child's development and the overall strength of the family. Secondly, the law mandates a statewide system of early intervention services rather than establishing specific services. Central to this delivery model is the establishment of Interagency Coordinating Councils (ICC's) charged with developing specific implementation procedures appropriate for the unique needs and resources of each state.

A myriad of services must now be made available, from birth on, to all children with special needs and their families. The provisions regulating these services will be differentially viewed as either a radical departure from previous policies or as an incremental change depending on one's perspective (Kraus, 1990). While traditionally, policies have maintained a hands-off approach to public intervention in the lives of families not otherwise identified as having problems, P.L. 99-457 requires that the child and family be viewed as a unit. This makes it possible, or necessary, depending on one's perspective, to address the needs of individuals as well as the family collectively, rather than separately. While this represents a departure from previous policies, it does reflect current principles of best practices.

Both parental involvement in child development programs and inter-agency cooperation have been encouraged in the past, primarily in family support and early childhood programs. Early childhood professionals contend that parental involvement in their children's programming is needed if maximum developmental gains are to be achieved and maintained (Welsh & Odum, 1981). A review of 21 early intervention projects provides evidence of this philosophy's widespread acceptance by revealing that 81% of these projects involved parents to a substantial degree (White, Mastropieri, & Casto, 1984).

Early intervention efforts aimed at supporting parents in their role as the child's primary teacher and care-giver and at strengthening the parent-child relationship appear to be particularly beneficial (Welsh & Odum, 1981). Additionally, efforts toward goals such as these would appear to be best supported by interagency cooperation. Now, as illustrated by the components of P.L. 99-457, both parental involvement and interagency cooperation in the design and delivery of services are mandated for all eligible children through age two.

REQUIREMENTS OF PUBLIC LAW 99-457

P.L. 99-457 contains 14 minimum requirements which must be uniformly followed throughout the nation. Listing these will help to illustrate the flexibility allowed states in the actual development of guidelines for services. The key components of P.L. 99-457, Part H, include the following:

1. Definition of developmental delay.
2. Timetable for availability of services.

3. Comprehensive multi-disciplinary evaluation of needs of children and families.

4. Individualized family service plan which includes case management services.

5. A comprehensive child-find and referral system.

6. Public awareness program to focus on early identification.

7. A central directory of services, resources, state experts, research and demonstration projects.

8. A comprehensive system of personnel development.

9. A single line of authority to a lead agency.

10. A policy for contracting or making arrangements with local service providers.

11. A procedure for timely reimbursement of funds.

12. Procedural safeguards specifying parental rights to consent, involvement in assessment and programming, and due process.

13. Policies and procedures for personnel standards.

14. A system for compiling data regarding the state's early intervention policies, programs, and services.

While the components of P.L. 99-457 provide general parameters for implementing the state's efforts many questions are, as yet, unanswered.

POLICY DEVELOPMENT AND IMPLEMENTATION

Passage of P.L. 99-457 created the impetus for each state to examine services currently being provided to young children and their families, and to plan future services considering the particular strengths and resources available in each individual state. This task was to be accomplished via the work of State Interagency Coordinating Councils.

The law recognizes the fact that early intervention services vary greatly from state to state. Therefore, states are allowed to capitalize on existing strengths, as well as on current and projected efforts in meeting the requirements of P.L. 99-457.

STATE ORGANIZATION

The first task in implementing P.L. 99-457 is for each state's governor to designate a Lead Agency and establish an Interagency Coordinating Council. States are allowed discretion with respect to designation of a Lead Agency, which is responsible for overall administration of the program/s. All states and the District of Columbia have designated a Lead Agency. The most frequently named are Education (20 states), Health (15 states), and Human Services (14 states). On average, every state listed 3 to 4 agencies with primary responsibility for managing services for young children (Meisels, Harbin, Modigliani & Olson, 1988).

The law also established Interagency Coordinating Councils. The Councils are to be composed of all relevant agencies providing services to young children, as well as representative consumers and providers. The Councils are charged with assisting in the development and implementation of state policies, and advising the state by providing such services as assistance with development of interagency agreements and identification of resources (ERIC, 1988).

Each state has been required, via the process outlined above, to adopt a public policy providing for all components of a statewide system for provision of early intervention services to eligible children and their families. To date, all states have begun work on implementing the requirements of P.L. 99-457.

IDENTIFICATION OF POPULATION TO BE SERVED

Regulations outlined in Part H of P.L. 99-457 were designed to support the development of state-wide systems to provide services to young children with special needs (Smith, 1988). This process requires two decisions related to defining the population to be served. First, the definition of developmental delay must be established to determine eligibility for services. Secondly, states are afforded the option of expanding eligibility criteria to serve children from risk categories.

Clearly, there is a direct relationship between the breadth of eligibility criteria and the number of children identified as eligible for service. Smith & Strain (1988) suggests that variations in definition of developmental delay could result in great differences - as much as 1% to 20% - in the prevalence of eligible children, between the ages of 0 and 2, identified as having special needs.

Following from this step is the relationship between numbers of children served and the amount of money available to fund services for each individual child. Under P.L. 99-457, services must be available to each child meeting the eligibility criteria. Current evidence indicates that funding for this legislation was based on estimates of children needing services which has already proven to be too low (Barnett, 1988). Thus, decisions about eligibility will ultimately determine not only the numbers of children receiving services, but also the types of services which may be available to each child.

SERVICE DELIVERY

Actual services will continue to vary considerably, in consideration of many factors ranging from the resources and needs of individual families, to previously established programs and procedures, and to the restrictions imposed by geographic location. P.L. 99-457 allows for maximum flexibility in both design and delivery of services. However, it is required that services to any family will be guided by an Individualized Family Service Plan (IFSP) and that a case manager will be named to assist each family through the implementation of that plan. In reality, IFSP's and the roles played by case managers will be, in and of themselves, a reflection of the extent to which the policies spelled out by P.L. 99-457 have been implemented.

Individualized Family Service Plans (IFSP's)

The Individualized Family Service Plan (IFSP) is patterned substantially after the Individualized Educational Plan (IEP) which has come to be seen as the document guiding the delivery of most special education services to children and youth with handicaps. An IFSP is very similar to an IEP; indeed, it contains many of the same features except for two primary characteristics. It outlines services to be provided to an entire family rather than only to the child(ren) with special needs, and it may call for those services to be provided by multiple agencies (Smith & Strain, 1988).

Like the IEP, an IFSP must be developed by an interdisciplinary team, with all involved parties being fairly represented before services may be initiated. Also like an IEP, it contains information about current functioning levels and developmental goals, although this information is provided for the family as well as the child. Methods to be used to measure progress, services and how those are to be provided, projected dates for implementing the service plan, and responsibility for monitoring the plan are also included.

According to P.L. 99-457, the IFSP must contain: (1) a statement of the child's present levels of development (cognitive, speech/language, psychosocial, motor, and self-help); (2) a statement of the family's strengths and needs related to enhancing the child's development; (3) a statement of major outcomes expected to be achieved for the child and family and the criteria, procedures, and time-lines for determining progress; (4) the specific early intervention services necessary to meet the unique needs of the child and family including the method, frequency, and intensity of services; (5) the projected dates for initiation of services and expected duration; (6) the name of the case manager who will be responsible for the implementation of the plan; and (7) procedures for transition from early intervention into a preschool program.

IMPLICATIONS FOR IMPLEMENTING IFSP'S

The development and implementation of IFSP's have many implications - both for the children and families who will be served and for the professionals working with families. The IFSP's specify the assessed strengths and needs of individual children and families, the actual services to be provided, providers of those services, procedures to be used, and persons responsible for monitoring the plan's progress.

Many challenges remain in implementing the requirements of the IFSP. Included are the development and dissemination of reliable and valid assessment instruments, the coordination of community resources in order to deliver services in an efficient manner, and the training of personnel to fill various roles. However, overarching all these is the apparent necessity to view early intervention as a collaborative process and work to make actual services reflect this perspective.

THEORETICAL OVERVIEW

If we are to fulfill the spirit of P.L. 99-457, the deficits model theory underlying much of special education is not likely to serve us well. This approach implies that families are not functioning adequately and are displaying deficits in need of remediation. It has two serious limitations for guiding service delivery. This model does not provide guidelines for resolving conflicts, which may arise as several needs, both within and across individual family members, are identified for intervention. Neither does it provide guidance in designing and selecting means for meeting needs. Identification of needs is only the first step toward meeting them, and the families to be served may often have several needs which all warrant intensive, systematic programming and thus, compete with one another for attention (Kaiser & Hemmeter, 1988).

In place of a needs-based model, many researchers have drawn upon the family systems perspective (Minuchin, 1974; 1985) and the values framework (Hobbs, Dokecki, Hoover-Dempsey, Moroney, Shayne & Weeks, 1984) to recommend both theoretical and procedural guidelines for current and future practice (Benson & Turnbull, 1986; Bristol & Gallagher, 1982; Dunst & Trivette, 1988; Dunst, Leet & Trivette, 1988; Dunst, 1985; Kaiser & Hemmeter, 1988; Odom, Yoder & Hill, 1988). This perspective is social and relational as opposed to being individual and absolute. Within this framework a family is more than a collection of individuals occupying a specific physical and psychological space together. Rather, it is a natural social system (Goldenberg & Goldenberg, 1980).

Extending the family systems model, individuals, families, schools, and society are all parts of a system. The "fit" between component parts is a critical concern. Family-based interventions then, must be designed to support optimal development of the target child and other family members, strengthen the family unit, and contribute to the good of the larger society. In addition, they must be in accord with the values of the family, the intervenor, and the agency employing the intervenor (Kaiser & Hemmeter, 1988). They must also reflect broad societal values such as that of full integration for people with disabilities.

SETTING PERSPECTIVES — CASE MANAGEMENT

Dunst, Trivette & Deal (1988) have been leaders in calling for what has been named an "enabling and empowering" approach to working with families. Their primary recommendation for moving this from theory to practice is to have case managers and interventionists adopt this attitude and reflect it in their work.

The enablement and empowerment approach assumes that individuals and families with special needs have existing strengths, as well as the capacity to become more competent (Dunst, Trivette & Deal, 1988). In addition, it encourages family members, both individually and collectively, to assume an active rather than passive role in the process and function as independently as possible. Case management within the enablement and empowerment approach, as in other approaches, does call for the integration and coordination of services and/or supports in response to individual and family needs but specifically emphasizes doing so in ways that empower family members to become as independent and self-sustaining as possible.

P.L. 99-457 states that an IFSP must name a case manager who will be responsible for implementing the plan and coordinating services with other agencies and persons. Case management generally refers to the functions needed to mobilize resources and meet individual and family needs (Austin, 1983). In large part, the role has evolved in response to rapid growth in human service programs that has often resulted in fragmented and uncoordinated services. Case management has received emphasis in the health and human service arenas, but it is a relatively unfamiliar concept for educational agencies (Odom, Yoder & Hill, 1988). Thus, clear guidelines for implementing quality case management services for very young children and their families have not yet been developed.

PROCEDURAL RECOMMENDATIONS

The enablement and empowerment approach to early intervention is clearly in alignment with the family systems perspective. It is further supported by special education research findings which have shown that parents do not want to have their roles delineated by others and that families often need multiple support services. Embracing this approach will necessitate a rethinking of commonly used procedures when developing IFSP's (Dunst, Trivette & Leet, 1988). According to these writers, if IFSP's are to function effectively, they must be fluid as opposed to static. That is, they must permit frequent modification of goals, methods, and outcomes in response to changing family needs and/or situations.

From research and clinical efforts, Dunst, Trivette & Deal (1988) have recommended some simple and specific procedures to be used in developing and implementing IFSP's. First, they suggest that family needs and projects be recorded continuously as they are identified. These should be stated in terms of expected outcomes and ordered according to the family's desire to meet the needs. Next, the sources of support to be mobilized to accomplish each goal, as well as the particular resource to be accessed from each individual or agency, should be listed. The actions to be taken in these efforts must be stated, and the roles family members will play emphasized. Finally, the results of intervention efforts need to be evaluated according to their effectiveness in meeting stated needs. Bennett, Lingerfelt & Nelson (1990) have developed a training manual to help providers understand and realize this enablement approach to IFSP development.

Bailey and his colleagues (1986) have made similar recommendations but have also addressed the potential need for an intervenor to target additional, or alternative, goals for a family. They recognize that situations may arise whereby a family is unable to see a particular problem due to attention on more immediate problems, where a family may be unable or unwilling to express a need, or where the needs of family members may actually be in conflict with the preferences of another member. In such cases, they suggest giving priority to family stated goals whenever possible in order to help establish trust and secure cooperation. However, they claim that in some cases interveners do have the responsibility to set alternate goals for families.

If the enablement and empowerment to early intervention services approach could be widely adopted, some important issues still remain to be resolved in the implementation of IFSP's.

Unresolved Issues

CASE MANAGEMENT AND INTERAGENCY COLLABORATION

Two integral and closely related issues are the mandate for interagency coordination and the naming of a case manager. P.L. 99-457 specifies that an individual most relevant to the needs of a child and family be designated as case manager and assume the additional responsibilities of service coordination (Campbell, Bellamy & Bishop, 1988). However, implicit in the action is the notion that neither this person nor his/her employing agency, necessarily serve as the only intervenor for a family. Rather appropriate and desired services are to be provided, in an efficient manner, by any number of agencies working in concert.

A basic framework for effective case management is suggested by Wray & Wieck (1985). It includes these five components: a well-defined process, clear designation of case responsibility, the availability of good information about clients and services, clear interagency agreements, and adequate resources. A recent study of case management for 169 children with special health care needs revealed, however, that these five elements were seldom all present (Patten, Martin, Lindahl, Hestness, Neinen, Threlkeld, Davies, 1989). These researchers found a substantial amount of informal coordination and linkage in the delivery of services which they suggest provides a positive base for further development of organized coordination activities.

Given case management's relatively untested role in early intervention and the fact that multiple perspectives on case management exist, Bailey (1989) has identified three issues needing further examination. These include deciding who should best serve as case manager, what skills case managers need, and what administrative authority case managers should be given.

Specific issues in naming a case manager will vary greatly in consideration of a particular child and family. Currently, arguments exist over whether direct interventionists, such as teachers and therapists, other professionals such as social workers, or parents can play the role most effectively (Bailey, 1989). Even though the law states that the case manager be from the profession most immediately relevant to the child's or family's needs, the fact that family members may often have multiple needs, does not necessarily make naming a case manager a simple task.

Skills needed and actual roles to be played for effective case management are closely related issues. By definition, case management will require the ability- both in terms of skills and administrative authority- to work across disciplines and settings (Smith, 1988). Case managers must be able to keep members of an interdisciplinary intervention team working together with each other and family members, and in addition must be able to access all family records among involved agencies, relevant for intervention. However, specific training competencies have not been identified to date, and guidelines on how case management will fit into the overall administrative hierarchy of early intervention programs have not been established (Bailey, 1989).

Interagency collaboration is not an entirely new concept, but like case management, has not been widely used within early intervention. As stated earlier, each state has a lead agency designated and an interagency coordinating council in place, but exactly what role these councils are to play is not known. What authority they have to secure the cooperation of various agencies is also not specifically outlined in P.L. 99-457, and these issues are expected to be resolved with time.

Some pioneer efforts at interagency collaboration have been documented and procedural recommendations given should prove helpful (Huntze, 1988). Guidelines have been provided for agencies to use in clarifying their own purposes, establishing communication lines, framing contracts, and evaluating procedures and services.

Analogous to the issue of interagency collaboration are those of service delivery and payment for services. Flexibility and responsiveness rather than consistency are recommended in order for services to be both individualized and efficient (Smith, 1988; McPherson, 1983). Again, documentation of practices are available, but widespread implementation of coordinated service practices to young children and their families is yet to come.

Smith (1988) provides an extensive list of references and resources which should prove helpful to program administrators responsible for securing resources to finance services. However as stated above, the U. S. Congress allocated funding for services based upon an estimate of need already documented as too low. Unfortunately, again service providers and policy makers may very well be forced to develop practical rules as they go along based upon the experiences they are soon to encounter.

Assessment and Evaluation

To accomplish the goals set forth in P.L. 99-457, assessment activities will also need to become family focused. Assessment of child and family needs and strengths, individually and as a family unit, as well as the evaluation of intervention effectiveness, are issues needing attention in this effort. Individualized programming requires careful documentation of children's development and the needs of families (Bailey & Simeonsson, 1984).

Bailey (1988) lists several functions which must be incorporated into an effective family assessment. First, it must cover important family domains and do so in a manner which recognizes the importance of family values. Family assessment must allow for the identification of family priorities for goals and services, vary according to the demands or type of program, and provide regular evaluation of family outcomes. An assessment such as this must incorporate information from multiple sources and measures.

Bailey (1988) also specifies the following five domains for examination in a family assessment: child needs and characteristics likely to affect family functioning, parent-child interactions, family needs, critical events, and family strengths. Efforts have been undertaken to develop instruments and procedures to assess each of these domains and also to evaluate intervention efforts. While many assessment instruments have been developed and used clinically, their technical properties vary greatly (Bailey & Simeonsson, 1988).

Only widespread implementation of family assessment measures will determine the extent to which this critical need has been addressed. Kraus (1990) suggests that developing standardized measurement of family functioning will be challenging as development of technically sound instruments may contribute to differences rather than resolve disagreements between parents and professionals in regard to both methodological relevance and sensitivity to issues of privacy and cultural differences.

Personnel Preparation

The critical shortage of adequately prepared personnel to deliver early intervention services has been well documented (Meisels, et. al., 1988; McLauglin, Smith-Davis & Burke, 1986; Harbin, 1988). Kraus (1990) states that local early intervention professionals are the "front-line" implementors of P.L. 99-457, and as such their training and experience, as well as the availability of effective assessment procedures and curriculum materials, will critically affect the implementation of this law. Efforts are underway to fill this need for personnel and several experienced researchers have developed both pre-service and in-service training programs (Bailey, et. al., 1988; Bricker & Slentz, 1985; Burke, McLaughlin & Valdivieso, 1988; Harbin, 1988). All stress the need for trans-disciplinary training and practice.

A review of 40 federally funded personnel preparation projects revealed that these programs have provided training for more than 1000 interventionists during the latter half of the 1980's (Bruder & McLean, 1988). These projects have concentrated on providing training to special educators, as well as related service personnel such as physical and occupational therapists, nurses, social workers, speech and language pathologists and psychologists.

Many of the training projects reviewed reflected the notion that infant intervention is a unique enterprise demanding training specific to the needs of infants and families (Bruder & McLean, 1988). Training requirements varied from project to project, but generally included both coursework and practicum experiences designed to build competencies in several areas including child development, family involvement, assessment, case management and teaming, program planning and administration, and evaluation.

There is also a need for leadership training in the field of early intervention. The ability to provide successful early intervention at the service level will depend on leadership and policies which are supportive of and conducive to comprehensive programs delivered via multi-disciplinary, interagency coordination. Training programs which are able to incorporate the specialized knowledge necessary to work effectively young children and their families, as well as the advanced knowledge and skills necessary to carry out critical leadership and decision making roles in administration, training, planning, policy analysis and development, and research are needed.

Conclusion

The full implementation of P.L. 99-457 will be a challenge for the next decade and beyond. At the present time, work continues in every state. Individual agencies are developing and implementing programs, interagency coordinating councils are meeting regularly, and local and state officials are forging policies to guide practice.

While P.L. 99-457 provides general parameters to guide early intervention efforts, many issues must be addressed if the needs of children and families are to be adequately met. Early intervention professionals, in concert with families and state and local agencies, must develop procedures for identification and assessment of children and families, implementation and monitoring of services including both direct intervention and case management, policy development and analysis, and personnel development.

Smith & Strain (1988) suggest that we look to ourselves, as professionals, rather than to the legislative arena to meet this challenge. Beginning steps should include monitoring implementation of P.L. 99-457 and related state policies, as well as being active in quality control efforts. Only this way can we assure that not only will the intent of the law be met, but that best practices will be incorporated and high quality services delivered to children and families.

References

Austin, C. D. (1983). Case management in long-term care: Options and opportunities. *Health and Social Work, 8,* 16-30.

Bailey, D. B. (1989). Case management in early intervention, *Journal of Early Intervention, 13(2),* 120-134.

Bailey, D. B. (1988). Rationale and model for family assessment in early intervention. In D. B. Bailey & R. J. Simeonsson (Eds.), *Family assessment in early intervention,* (pp. 1-26), Columbus: Merrill Publishing Co.

Bailey, D. B., & Simeonsson, R. F. (1984). Critical issues underlying research and intervention with families of young handicapped children. *Journal of the Division for Early Childhood, 8,* 38-48.

Bailey, D. B., & Simeonsson, R. J. (1988). Home-based early intervention. In S.L. Odom & M. B. Karnes (Eds.), *Early intervention for infants and children with handicaps: An empirical base,* Baltimore: Paul H. Brookes.

Bailey, D. B., Simeonsson, R. J., Winton, P. J., Huntington, G. S., Comfort, M., Isbell, P., O'Donnell, K. J., & Helm, J. M. (1986). Family-focused intervention: A functional model for planning, implementing, and evaluating individualized family services in early intervention. *Journal of the division for Early Childhood, 10,* 156-171.

Barnett, S. W. (1988). The economics of preschool special education under public law 99-457. *Topics in Early Childhood special education, 8(1),* 12-23.

Bennett, T., Lingerfelt, B.V., Nelson, D.E. (1990). *Developing Individualized Family Support Plans: A Training Manual,* Cambridge, MA: Brookline Books.

Benson, H. A., & Turnbull, A. P. (1986). Approaching families from an individualized perspective. In R. H. Homer, L. H. Meyers, & H. D. Fredericks (Eds.), *Education of Learners with Severe Handicaps: Exemplary Service Strategies* (pp. 127-157). Baltimore: Paul H. Brookes.

Bloom, B. (1964). *Stability and change in human characteristics,* New York: Wiley.

Bricker, D., & Casuso, V. (1979). Family involvement: A critical component of early intervention. *Exceptional Children, 46,* 108-116.

Bricker, D., & Slentz, K. (1985). Personnel preparation: Handicapped infants. In M. C. Wang, M. C. Reynolds, & H. J. Walberg (Eds.), *Handbook of special education: Research and practice (Vol. 3).* Elmsford, NY: Pergamon Press.

Bristol, M. M., & Gallagher, J. J. (1982). A family focus for intervention. In C. Ramey & P. L. Trohavis (Eds.), *Finding and educating high-risk and handicapped infants* (pp. 137-162). Baltimore: University Park Press.

Bronfenbrenner, U. (1974). Is early intervention effective? *Teachers College Record, 76(2)*, 279-303.

Bruder, M. B., & McLean, M. (1988). Personnel Preparation for Infant Interventionists: A Review of Federally Funded Projects. *Journal of the Division for Early Childhood, 12 (4)*, 299-305.

Burke, P. J., McLaughlin, M. J., & Valdivieso, C. H. (1988). Preparing professionals to educate handicapped infants and young children: Some policy considerations. *Topics in Early Childhood Special Education, 8,* 73-80.

Campbell, P. H., Bellamy, G. T., & Bishop, K. K. (1988). Statewide intervention systems: An overview of the new federal program for infants and toddlers with handicaps, *The Journal of Special Education, 22,* 25-40.

Dunst, C. J., Trivette, C. M., & Deal, A. (1988). *Enabling and empowering families: Principles and guidelines for practice.* Cambridge, MA: Brookline Books.

Dunst, C. J., & Trivette, C. M. (1988). An enablement and empowerment perspective of case management. *Topics in Early Childhood Special Education, 8,* 87-102.

Dunst, C. J., Leet, HJ. E., & Trivette, C. M. (1988). Family resources, personal well-being, and early intervention. *The Journal of Special Education, 22,* 108-116.

Dunst, C. J. (1985). Rethinking early intervention. *Analysis and Intervention in Developmental Disabilities, 5,* 165-201.

Erickson, M. F., Sroufe, L. A., & Egeland, B. (1985). The relationship between quality of attachment and behavior problems in preschool in a high-risk sample. In I. Bretherton and E. Waters (Eds.), *Monographs for the Society for Research in Child Development, 50,* 147-166.

Foster, M., Berger, M., & McLean, M. (1981). Rethinking a good idea: A reassessment of parent involvement. *Topics in Early Childhood Special Education, 1(3),* 55-65.

Goldenberg, I., & Goldenberg, H. (1980). *Family therapy: An overview.* Monterey, CA: Brooks/Cole Publishing Co.

Goodson, B. D., & Hess, R. D. *Parents as teachers of young children: An evaluative review of some contemporary concepts and programs.* Washington, D.C.: Bureau of Educational Personnel Development, DHEW/OE, 1975. (ERIC Document Reproduction Service No. ED 136 967).

Gray, S. W. (1971). The child's first teacher. *Childhood Education, 48(3),* 127-129.

Harbin, G. L. (1988). Implementation of P. L. 99-457: State technical assistance needs. *Topics in Early Childhood Special Education, 8,* 24-36.

Healy, A., Keesee, P. D., & Smith, B. S. (1985). *Early services for children with special needs: Transactions for family support.* Iowa City: University of Iowa.

Hobbs, N., Dokecki, P. R., Hoover-Dempsey, K. V., Moroney, R. M., Shayne, M.W., & Weeks, K. H. (1984). *Strengthening families.* San Francisco: Jossey-Bass.

Hunt, J. McV. (1961). *Intelligence and experience.* New York: Ronald Press.

Huntze, S. L. (1988). Cooperative interface of schools and other child care systems for behaviorally disordered students. In M. C. Wang, M. C. Reynolds, & H. J. Walberg (Eds.), *Handbook of special education: Research and practice (Vol. 2)* (pp. 195-217). New York: Pergamon Press.

Kaiser, A. P., & Hemmeter, M. L. (1988). Value-based approaches to family intervention. *Topics in Early Childhood Special Education, 8,* 72-86.

Krauss, M. W. (1990). New precedent in family policy: Individualized family service plan. *Exceptional Children, 56(5),* (pp. 388-395).

Lillie, D. L. (1975). The parent in early childhood education. *Journal of Research and Development ion Education, 8(2),* 7-12.

McLaughlin, M. J., Smith-Davis, J., & Burke, P. J. (1986). *Personnel to educate the handicapped in America: A status report.*College Park: University of Maryland.

McPherson, M. (1983). Improving services to infants and young children with handicapping conditions and their families: The Division of Maternal and Child Health as collaborators. *Zero to Three, 4,* 1-6.

Meisels, S. J., Harbin, G., Modligliani, K., & Olson, K. (1988). Formulating optimal state early childhood intervention policies. *Exceptional Children, 55,* 159-162.

Minuchin, P. (1985). Families and individual development: Provocations from the field of family therapy. *Child Development, 56,* 289-302.

Minuchin, P. (1974). *Families and family therapy.* Cambridge, MA: Howard University Press.

Odom, S. L., Yoder, P., & Hill, G. (1988). Developmental intervention for infants with handicaps: Purposes and programs. *The Journal of Special Education, 22,* 11-24.

Patten, S. K., Martin, M., Lindahl-Hestness, L., Heinen, M. J., Threlkeld, C. & Davies, N. (1989). *A study of case management for children with special health care needs.* Unpublished manuscript, University of Minnesota, Division of Maternal and Child Health.

Ramey, C. T., Bell, P. B., & Gowen, J. W.(1980). Parents as educators during infancy: Implications from research for handicapped infants. In J. J. Gallagher (Ed.), *New directions in exceptional children,* (pp. 59-84). San Francisco, CA: Jossey-Bass.

Smith, B. (Ed.). (1988). *Mapping the future for children with special needs: P. L. 99-457.*Iowa City, IA: University of Iowa.

Smith, B. J., & Strain, P. S. (1988). Early childhood special education in the next decade: Implementing and expanding P. L. 99-457. *Topics in Early Childhood Special Education, 8,* 37-47.

Turnbull, A. P., & Winton, P. J. (1984). Parent involvement policy and practice: Current future and perspectives. In J. Blacher (Ed.), *Young severely handicapped children and their families: Research in review.* (pp. 377-397). New York: The Free Press.

Valentine, J., & Stark, E. (1979). The social context of parent involvement in Head Start. In E. Zigler & J. Valentine (Eds.), *Project Head Start* (pp.291-313). New York: The Free Press.

Welsh, M. M., & Odum, C. S. (1981). Parent involvement in the education of the handicapped child: A review of the literature, *Journal of the Division for Early Childhood, 3(1),* 15-25.

White, K. R., & Casto, G. (1989). What is known about early intervention. In C. Tingey (Ed.), *Implementing Early Intervention* (pp. 3-20). Baltimore, MD: Paul H. Brooks Publishing Co.

White, K. R., Mastropieri, M., & Casto, G. (1984). An analysis of special education early childhood projects approved by the joint dissemination review panel, *Journal of the Division for Early Childhood,* 11-26.

Wray, L, & Wieck, C. (1985). Moving Persons with Developmental Disabilities toward Less Restrictive Environments through Case Management. In K. C. Lakin & R. H. Bruininks (Eds.), *Strategies for achieving community integration of developmentally disabled citizens,*(pp. 219-230). Paul H. Brookes.

Yawkey, T. D., & Bakawa-Evenson, L. (1975). The child care professional-parent child: An emerging triad. *Child Care Quarterly, 4(4),* 172-179.

Zantal-Wiener, K. (1988). *Preschool services for children with handicaps.* (Report No. 400-84-0010). Reston, VA: Clearinghouse on Handicapped and Gifted Children. (ERIC Digest No. 450).

CHAPTER X

Case Management: A New Challenge for Families

Thomas J. Zirpoli, College of St. Thomas

Colleen Wieck, Minnesota Governor's Planning Council on Developmental Disabilities

Marijo McBride, Institute on Community Integration, University of Minnesota

"Service Delivery should support not supplant the family"
(Edward Skarnulis, 1982)

Advocacy and service delivery systems for persons with developmental disabilities and their families have, in some ways, usurped the place of the family. At the very least, these systems have decreased the significance of the parents' role as *primary provider* in the life of their children. Frequently, these systems have placed persons with disabilities and their families in passive roles with few opportunities to express their needs, review alternatives, and make decisions regarding their own future.

Perhaps one primary reason for this intrusion is an outdated, but still prevalent perception of persons with disabilities and their families as unable to care for themselves and in need of external protection, assistance, and advocacy. In addition, families have always been encouraged to seek *professional* guidance and assistance for most aspects of a disabled family member's life.

The institutionalization of persons with disabilities provides a good example. How were families encouraged to send their children out of the home, away from the family? The perception was that persons with disabilities had special needs that could not be provided by untrained parents. Indeed, parents of persons with disabilities have historically been encouraged to put aside their instincts about what they perceive as best for their sons and daughters and follow, without question, the advice of professionals.

CRITERIA FOR CHOOSING A CASE MANAGER

It is generally recognized, by law and in practice, that parents are legitimate members of a *team* of individuals responsible for servivce plans. However, it is almost always assumed that the *team leader* or *case manager* will be selected from the professional members of the team. This person may be the social worker, educator, or developmental specialist, but never the individual and seldom the family.

Morton (1988) outlined several criteria for the selection of a person's case manager. Below some of these criteria are outlined and reviewed in light of a parent's qualifications to be the case manager, below.

The intensity of involvement. This is clearly an important variable in the selection of a case manager. Indeed, the case manager should be the member of the team who is the most involved with the individual and the individual's family.

In most cases, it is the parents who have the greatest intensity of involvement. This is not a slight to the caring and dedicated work of many public case managers. However, the typical heavy case load of many public case managers prohibits a high intensity of involvement for any one case.

The number and variety of services needed by the child and family. Parents of children with disabilities frequently must learn how to be expert coordination specialists. They must coordinate all the educational and medical services needed by the family member. In addition, these services are usually provided by different state, city, and/or county agencies. Even when a public case manager has the authority for coordination, parents usually end up with the responsibility for ensuring that a family member is getting what is needed. A review of special education history clearly points to the role of parents as the significant advocates for change. Parents, not public case managers or other public advocates, have typically shouldered the burden of legislative and court battles. Many students with disabilities would not be receiving appropriate services today if not for the advocacy of their parents.

The preference of the family. Parents are seldom allowed to choose their child's case manager. Frequently, the case manager is identified in advance of team meetings, without any discussion by team members, including parents, as to who would best serve as the case manager. Although it is recognized that some parents may not want to serve as their child's case manager, parents should at least have the option to accept or reject the responsibility.

Accessibility to the family. According to Morton (1988), accessibility is "based upon a 'match' between child and family and the professional" (p. 13). Although an individual professional may have frequent contact with family members, he or she may be a poor 'match' in terms of real responsiveness to the family's life. This is a significant issue for the family that must build a trusting relationship with the professional who will serve as the official service coordinator for their family member.

PARENTS AS CASE MANAGERS

"Case management is inherently a simple service- finding out what a family needs and helping them get it" (Morton, 1988, p. 13)

Parents are frequently placed in the position of knowing what services they need but having to depend upon others to ensure that their child will receive those services. The problems involved in getting appropriate services involve several issues. First, many parents don't know what services are available to them. Second, many parents don't know what their legal rights are regarding the acquisition of specific services. Third, many parents don't have the skills to advocate for their disabled children to ensure that their children receive appropriate services.

Fortunately, a growing number of public and private organizations are providing parents with the knowledge and skills necessary to identify community services, recognize their legal rights regarding those services, and advocate for the provision of appropriate services for their family. The objective of these programs include teaching parents how to be self-advocates and their own family case manager by first learning how the system works and then learning how to effectively use the system.

As self-advocates and case managers, parents are empowered to identify, communicate, and obtain services necessary to meet their family needs. They learn that they don't have to depend upon others to speak for them on issues affecting their lives (Vitello & Soskin, 1985).

Two such programs, **Parent Case Management (PCM)** and **Partners in Policymaking (Partners),** are outstanding examples of parent education and training programs whose goals are to provide parents with the knowledge and skills necessary to become parent case managers and self-advocates. These two programs based in Minnesota are considered model parent training programs. They are based upon a philosophy that views individuals and parents as the most significant member of the team. Both programs are described here to enable replication in other states.

Parent Case Management Project

"Parents learned the system of services as they used those services while depending on the professionals and providers of that information. This dependency facilitated the juxtaposition of leadership from the parent to the professional, be it the case manager or a vendor of service" (Thinesen, McBride, & Lang, 1988, p. 3)

Parents of children with developmental disabilities living in suburban counties of Minneapolis and St. Paul, Minnesota participated in a program designed to teach parents how to be case managers for their children. This model was proposed as an alternative to the current county case management system used in Minnesota. In order to evaluate the effectiveness of this program, the parent case managers were compared to two control groups. The first control group included parents who did not participate in the training program or who had very limited exposure to the PCM training. The second control group consisted of public case managers from the local community; some of the public case managers attended some of the PCM training workshops.

PARTICIPANTS

In the first year of the PCM project, the twelve parent participants were solicited through newspaper and newsletter ads, public service announcements, and phone calls. Parents in the control group (n=9) were selected from the local ARC mailing list. These parents had children with similar disabilities to those of the 12 parents who received the PCM training. The public case managers in the second control group consisted of eight county case managers from the local community who agreed to participate in the project. The county case managers were all college graduates, had been case managers for an average of 7.4 years (range= 2.5 to 10 years), and served an average case load of 44.8 clients.

CASE MANAGEMENT TRAINING AND PRACTICE

Parents participating in the PCM project attended workshops throughout the project. Some workshops were open to the public and, as previously stated, a few members of both control groups attended some of these workshops. Training was presented by officials from the Minnesota Department of Human Services, psychologists, professional advocates, and others. Workshops were presented over a 7 month period in the form of lectures, discussions, and readings. Each parent in the PCM training group was required to participate in a minimum of 40 hours of training. Actual participation averaged 60 hours per parents (range= 41-99 hours).

In addition to other instructional reading materials, participants were provided with a Parent Case Management Training Manual, developed during the project. Also, a scholarship fund administered by the local ARC provided funds for participants to attend training provided in the community. Also available from the local ARC were library materials and other resources, including personnel, to answer questions and assist in locating instructional materials.

Training topics included assertiveness, assessment of needs and services, legal issues, Individual Service Plans, networking, relationships with professionals, service delivery systems, and goals and objectives. In addition to the training offered by the project, participants attended public workshops provided by other agencies. For example, class catalogs and schedules from a number of local colleges and universities were made available to program participants. These provided additional training on topics such as assertiveness, futures planning, co-dependency, supported employment, living arrangements, and other issues related to services for persons with disabilities.

In addition to training, parents in the experimental group were paired with their child's current county case manager and assumed the role as Parent Case Managers for their children. During the development of the child's Individual Service Plan, the Parent and County co-managers negotiated and divided tasks and responsibilities. As case managers, parents played a greater role in the development of their child's Individual Service Plan, monitored services, identified available services, advocated and lobbied on issues concerning their family, collected progress data, and presented testimony to various groups and agencies.

In many cases, parents were given responsibilities for tasks they were already doing. Significantly, some parents assumed more active roles than others. As a symbol of the parents' new professional role and to help cover some expenses, the Parent Case Managers received a stipend of $40.00 per month for the 6 months of their training and practice.

EVALUATION

The project made comparisons among the 12 parents who participated in the Parent Case Management (PCM) Project, nine parents who had limited or no participation in the PCM training, and eight county case managers who had limited or no participation in the PCM training.

A pre- and post-test questionnaire was completed by members of all three groups. The confidential questionnaire was used to collect demographic data on all participants, along with questions regarding attitudes about parents as case managers. Some of the project research questions and results are outlined below.

RESULTS

"You can fool all of the people some of the time and some of the people all the time, but you can never fool a mother" (Wieck, 1989, p. 16).

What effect would parents as case managers have on services for their family and children? Perhaps the most important outcome variable-this study identified a 3.6 increase in the number of services received per family, on pre- to post-project measures, for the experimental group. This is compared to a 2.8 increase in the number of services received for the parent control group.

Would compensation and training lead to a decrease in stress and "burnout?" Parents who participated in the PCM training reported a slight decrease in levels of stress from pre- to post-test measures.

Following training would parents feel they could effectively exercise their natural authority? Compared to pretest measures, parents in the experimental group rated themselves slightly higher on this variable after their participation in the PCM training. The parent control group did not show a similar increase.

What duties and relationships would change between parents and county case managers when parents assumed the case management role? Parents stated more strongly than county case managers that parent case management should be supported. The county case managers indicated that the duties remained the same but their relationships with parents changed positively and that parents and case managers worked more effectively as a team. Eleven parents indicated a greater interest in being case managers following training and 1 reported no change. In the parent control group, only 1 parent indicated a greater interest and 4 indicated less interest.

What system changes would be identified as necessary to fully implement parent case management? Three primary changes were identified in response to this question. First, county guidelines that identify the county as the provider of case management were considered the most significant problem. Second, guidelines regarding the allocation of monetary resources and the lack of funding were identified as problematic. Last, a major system change identified to improve the opportunity for parent case managers is the ability for parents to authorize services. Currently, the system empowers professionals, not parents, to authorize services.

Would the Individual Service Plan developed by parent case managers be age appropriate, teach functional skills, and be community referenced? Ratings provided by both parents and county case managers indicated satisfaction with ISP's developed by parents. Parents generally completed more assessment areas, identified more needed services, and wrote goals and objectives that were more behaviorally based than the control groups.

Would parent case management training improve the parents' knowledge about the field of developmental disabilities? Scores on pre- and post-knowledge tests for 9 out of the 12 parent case managers indicated a post-test increase in knowledge about the field. Scores from two parents stayed the same and one decreased. Scores for the parent control group decreased slightly from pre to post-test, and scores for the county case managers were stable across pre- and post-tests. Pre- and post-test scores for all three groups are outlined in Table 10-1.

Parents reported that their greater level of knowledge made them more comfortable in working with their children, eased the feeling of "helplessness," and helped them establish support networks.

Partners in Policymaking

"The emergence of legal rights for 'persons with disabilities' has led to expectations that advocates will be available to defend those rights" (Herr, 1983, p. 211).

The availability of advocacy services for persons with disabilities and their families has not kept pace with demand (Herr, 1983; Vitello & Soskin, 1985). Persons with disabilities and their families have historically depended upon others to advocate on their behalf. However, as family members become more knowledgeable about available services and their rights to obtain those services, they become more empowered and learned in how to be self-advocates.

    Partners In Policymaking (Partners) was designed to provide advocacy education and training for persons with disabilities and their families so that they may obtain appropriate services, develop leadership potential, and impact on public policy (see Zirpoli, Hancox, Wieck, & Skarnulis, 1989). Many public and private organizations that once provided primary advocacy services now see self-advocacy training as an appropriate and beneficial service. One program, Partners in Policymaking, based in St. Paul, Minnesota, served as a model empowerment and self-advocacy training program. Partners in Policymaking was a federally funded, 3 year program with an annual budget of $100,000. The program was directed and staffed primarily through the Minnesota Governor's Planning Council on Developmental Disabilities (GPCDD). An overview of this program, along with some outcome data from first-year graduates, is provided below.

TABLE 10-1
Knowledge About the Disabilities Field-Test Results

True/False Test Results

	N	Pre-test	Post-test
Parent Case Managers	12	6.7	8.7
Control Group Parents	9	5.3	4.8
County Case Managers	8	9.4	9.4

Multiple Choice Test Results

	N	Pre-test	Post-test
Parent Case Managers	12	5.7	6.8
Control Group Parents	9	4.2	4.2
County Case Manager	8	7.8	6.9

PARTICIPANTS

Thirty-five participants were selected from a pool of applicants to participate in the first year of training of the Partners program. Thirty of the participants were parents of young children with disabilities and 5 were adults with disabilities. The mean age of the participants was 36 years. The mean age of their children with disabilities was 6.5 years.

An important component of the Partners program was the provision of support for the participants, in order to encourage participation, such as coverage of travel, meals, lodging, respite care, and child care expenses. In return, participants were asked to sign a contract regarding training attendance, homework assignments and other projects during the year-long training program.

ADVOCACY TRAINING AND PRACTICE

Training in the Partners program consisted of three main components. First, the core of the program consisted of eight 2-day training sessions or 16 total days of direct instruction. Training sessions began on Fridays after 12:00 noon and concluded late Saturday afternoon. Each training session included guest speakers on a variety of subjects including history, best practices, federal and local policymaking, services for persons with disabilities, advocacy and advocacy organizations, integration, and other topics. In addition, the participants visited state and federal officials, agencies and advocacy organizations.

The second component of Partners involved self-instruction that consisted of the distribution of reading materials, homework assignments, personal contacts with local, state, and federal policymakers, attendance at meetings and conferences, and presentations about the concerns of persons with disabilities. The third component of Partners involved the completion of a major project such as completing an internship, organizing meetings with officials, and so on.

EVALUATION

The evaluation component of Partners consisted of two parts. First, participants were asked to evaluate each weekend training session by completing a prepared evaluation form distributed at the end of each session.

Second, Partners organizers collected both pre- and post-training data on the type and quantity of advocacy activities completed by participants. Pre-training data was collected soon after the initiation of training and consisted of each participant completing a survey regarding their advocacy activities prior to training. Post-training data was collected 6 months after participants graduated from the program and consisted of each participant completing a survey regarding the type and quantity of advocacy activities they engaged in during the 6 month period immediately after graduation. The pre- and post-training data were compared as one measure of the effectiveness of the Partners program. In addition, participants were once again given an opportunity to evaluate the entire program by completing a survey mailed to them.

RESULTS

"Advocacy by as well as for persons with disabilities is now a reality" (Herr, 1983, p. 229).

On a scale of 1 to 5, with 5 being the maximum score, participants responded with a mean evaluation score of 4.40 for all training sessions with a range of 4.18 to 4.66 for individual sessions. On the 6 month follow-up survey, 57% of the participants rated the program as "excellent," 37% as "very good," and 6% as "good." Also, 82% stated that "I was very prepared," and 17% responded with "I was somewhat prepared," when asked how the Partners program prepared them to be effective advocates.

Regarding advocacy activities, all post-training measures were higher than pre-training measures. For example, post-training measures indicated that 80% of participants were serving on a committee or commission, 68% had been in contact with national officials, 83% had been in contact with state and local officials, and 57% had made office visits to public officials. These and other advocacy activities by Partners graduates during the 6 month period after graduation are outlined in Table 10-2.

Summary

The Parent Case Management project demonstrated that, when given the opportunity, some parents may welcome the chance to serve as their child's case manager. In this study, parents were paired with public county case managers and, as a result, their children received more services, parents felt empowered, more knowledgeable, and less stressed following their participation in the project. And the county case managers pointed to a more positive, cooperative working relationship with parents as a result of the project.

The use of parents as case managers, augmented by the provision of appropriate training and support, is seen by many as a workable model. In many cases, this model simply legitimizes the role parents already play in obtaining and coordinating the delivery of services for their children.

Partners in Policymaking has completed training for two additional groups of parents and adults with disabilities during 2 more years of funding. Results from these 2 years of advocacy training are as promising as they were from year one. Significantly, representatives from many states have expressed an interest in replicating this program in their home states.

Both of these programs challenge the traditional role of family members within developmental disabilities systems. Both programs are based upon the understanding that parents are significant members, if not the most

TABLE 10-2
*Advocacy Activities by Year 1 Participants During 6-Month
Period After Graduation From Partners Program*

Activity	Number of Participants	Percentage of Participants
Level of contract		
National officials	24	68.6
State officials	29	82.9
Local officials	29	82.9
No contact	2	5.7
Type of contact with public officials		
Letters	24	68.6
Phone calls	32	91.4
Office visits	20	57.1
Testimony public hearings	4	11.4
Serve on committee/commission	28	80.0
Other advocacy efforts reported		
Published articles/letters	15	42.9
Conference presentations	13	37.1
Presentations-other parents	10	28.6
TV/Radio appearances	3	8.6
Video presentations	3	8.6
On-the-job presentations	3	8.6

significant member, of any case planning team. These programs help
professionals to view parents in a new way as they challenge and invite
parents to be empowered and take charge.

References

Herr, S.S. (1983). *Rights and advocacy for retarded people*. Lexington, MA:
Lexington Books.

Michigan State Planning Council for Developmental Disabilities, (1982).
Guidelines for a life services system: Executive brief. Michigan State
University, East Lansing, Michigan.

Morton, D.R. (1988). Case management for early intervention services. *Family Support Bulletin.* United Cerebral Palsy Associations. Washington, DC.

Skarnulis, E. (1982). *Guidelines for a life services system: Executive brief.* Michigan State Planning Council for Developmental Disabilities.

Thinesen, P.J., McBride, M., & Lang, J.(1988). *An Evaluation of the effectiveness of the parent case management project.* Minnesota Governor's Planning Council on Developmental Disabilities, St. Paul, Minnesota.

Vitello, S.J., & Soskin, R.M. (1985). *Mental retardation: Its social and legal context.* NJ: Prentice-Hall, Inc.

Wieck, C. (1989). The development of family support programs. In J.M. Levy, P.H. Levy, & B. Nivin (Eds.), *Strengthening families.* NY: Young Adult Institute Press.

Zirpoli, T.J., Hancox, D., Wieck, C., & Skarnulis, E.R. Partners in policymaking: Empowering people. *Journal of the Association for Persons with Severe Handicaps. 14*, 163-167.

CHAPTER XI

Issues in Case Management for the '90's

Edward R. Skarnulis. Ph.D.

W hat is clear from the preceding chapters is that different people have different definitions, different expectations, different beliefs about what this thing called case management is, and what it was intended to do. Case management, however defined, has been in existence long enough to warrant an appraisal of how well it does what it was intended to do. But what are the measures of effectiveness, the standards against which we judge its performance. What changes if any, need to be made? This chapter attempts to summarize some of those recurring issues in case management that may need resolution if it is to be of maximum benefit to people with disabilities.

BACK TO BASICS

During the early 1970's I worked in a regional program called the Eastern Nebraska Community Office of Retardation (ENCOR), during a Camelot-like era when we had fairly flexible funding, strong local government support, and a lot of children of the '60's staff who were idealistic enough to believe that anything was possible. ENCOR during that time was a veritable "Who's Who" of some of the most talented, creative people in the field of developmental disabilities. Wolf Wolfensberger, Linda Glenn, Bob Perske, Karen Green-McGowan, Wade Hitzing, Frank Menolascino, Karen Faison, Brian Lensink, Shirley Dean, Bonnie Shoultz, Charlie Galloway, Patty Smith, Lois Rood, ... just some of a long list of people who made, and continue to make, enormous contributions to this work. From 1968 to 1975 these individuals designed and implemented integrated pre-schools, work stations in industry/enclaves, Program Analysis of Service Systems (PASS) evaluation methods, Pilot Parents, staffed apartments, equipment/toy lending libraries, Citizen Advocacy, and actualized the concept of zero reject by creating an array of services for those people who conventional professional wisdom of the time said could never leave institutions, i.e., those with severe behavior problems or medical needs.

The elements of what is now called *case management* were contained in a 1968 document that became the ENCOR blueprint, entitled, "The Initiation and Development of a Comprehensive, County-wide System of Services for the Mentally Retarded of Douglas County (Nebraska)." Among other things, it described services for children and adults with mental retardation which would be provided by a Family Evaluation and Guidance Service Section (Governor's Citizens Committee on Mental Retardation, 1968). Those services included intake and evaluation, service coordination, advocacy, guidance, friendship, emotional support, counselling and in-home support. Initially the staff were called guidance counselors, however the name was subsequently changed to advisor, in part to avoid a mental health, "sick person" role perception associated with medical model delivery system of the past.

ENCOR staff and parents were dedicated to bringing everyone home from the institution, using the concept of normalization as the value or standard against which all service delivery decisions would be made. It was a critical mass of people who believed in a Gestalt approach to service delivery, an appreciation of the wholeness of the person and ongoing complex social systems (Blanck and Turner, 1987), or what Lipsky calls an "Ecological Perspective." They felt that a human being's total environment, physical and interpersonal, was much more important than the intermittent clinical interventions of professionals in the lives of citizens with disabilities.

John McGee was also one of this group. John has distinguished himself by demonstrating that it is possible to help people labelled severely mentally retarded who exhibit what is euphemistically called "challenging behaviors," without having to resort to punishment. He was one of the most articulate spokespersons to argue for recognition of the importance of human relationships, of alienation or bonding, in the causation or extinguishing of self-destructive acts.

A few years ago this gentle man shared with me his frustration with people who were criticizing his work, people he characterized as "latter day saints of Normalization." What disappointed him most was the failure of others to distinguish between issues at the margins and what Burton Blatt called the quintessential issues. What was important was the determination to stop inflicting pain on other human beings, to stop dehumanization—an effort that still has not resulted in the elimination of aversive consequences. They continue to be used and defended by well known professionals in developmental disabilities.

Sometimes, in the rush to be a little more futuristic than our colleagues, a little more cutting edge, we behave *as though what should be already is.* Thus, although over 90,000 children and adults remain in institutions, and while Jerry Provencal exhorts others to have a sense of "passion," of urgency, about getting them out, many leaders have declared victory and gone home. Although the majority of children with disabilities are still in segregated schools and segregated classrooms, the program content of some of our national conferences would lead an outsider to believe that total integration had been achieved. Thus, although truly integrated jobs for adults with the most severe disabilities are almost non-existent in the United States, and many of those adults are on waiting lists for congregate, segregated settings (their families make a compelling case that something is better than nothing), the literature of our journals does not reflect the urgency of that need.

> As I see it, whether out of strategic necessity or the absence of better alternatives, advocates, like clinical professionals, have often been guilty of measuring out the lives of their clients in coffee spoons, as T.S. Eliot would describe it. While clinical professionals devote enormous resources to elaborate measurements of minute gains in learning, advocates often content themselves with equally small improvements for large efforts—e.g., moving clients from an open ward to one which is partitioned for more privacy; replacing old institutional buildings with newer ones; moving from a large institution to a smaller "community" ICF of 50 or 30 or 12 beds (Sundram, 1989).

Similarly, case management as it was envisioned for most children and adults and their families still does not exist. That must be the primary issue for the '90's. Even in states where it is provided, the case managers often have case loads of 1:50 or more, making it impossible to provide the services required. Thus, a central concern in case management for the next decade must be to not operate *as though what should be already is.*

ROLES OF CASE MANAGERS

One of the more obvious difficulties of setting up a good case management program is getting agreement on what case management should be. At the risk of over-simplification, case management roles generally fall within four categories: (1) the case manager as a partner and friend; (2) the case manager as a fiscal agent; (3) the case manager as a broker or service coordinator; and (4) the case manager as monitor and enforcer. In "Case Management: A New Challenge For Families." and in Betty Pendler's "Case Management Through the Life Cycle," the expectation was of the case manager as a partner, supporter and friend to parents and their sons and daughters with disabilities. On the other hand, the Novak, McAnally, Linz "Research Review" chapter describes the perspective of case management as a method of cost control:

> With the proliferation and the increased cost of services, the complexity of the service system multiplied.... potentially, large deficits in state Medicaid budgets for long term care have also forced many state budget personnel, human services, and Medicaid directors to seek ways to control costs... Hence, case management has been viewed as a key element in cost control (Simpson, 1982).

Allan Bergman, in "Content and Politics..." describes the role of case manager primarily as a service coordinator: "We need to call it what it is, or what it should be, which is 'service coordination'." Robert McDonald emphasizes the same need for coordination in his "Search for One-Stop Shopping." Perhaps because he is an attorney, Granquist has emphasized the responsibility of the case manager to enforce rules and regulations, to advocate on behalf of the person with disabilities to carry out mandates established in rule and law, to monitor and assure that the highest possible quality of services are delivered to consumers. Using somewhat different terminology to describe the four role expectations Wray calls attention to the ambiguities that exist:

> Clearly, from this definition, much more is expected from the case management system than the minimal brokerage role definition of case management often seen today. Case management systems are increasingly being asked to respond to the need for... tight monitoring of service delivery to individuals, the need to provide leadership for individual program planning, the need to provide a point of financial control and accountability for federal, state, and local funds, and the need to effectively advocate...

THE CASE MANAGER AS PARTNER

Betty Pendler wanted an interpreter, someone who could help her understand this strange new language, this medico-socio-psycho culture that was alien to anything she had ever known. She looked for someone to be her guide, to help her wend her way through the maze of bureaucracy, of regulations, of eligibility requirements. She wanted someone who could relieve her of the endless forms and paperwork, so that she could be free to concentrate her energy on the needs of her child. She sought someone who wouldn't say: "that's not my job," the kind of human being who isn't too good to roll up shirtsleeves, if need be, and help scrub a floor, feed a child, drive to the doctor's office, or make a run to the grocery store. A partner. An equal. Betty appreciated the importance of the "good housekeeping seals," the certificates and degrees and licenses of a professional which qualified them to move in the circles of other professionals and so get information and resources. But she also wanted somebody with "street savvy" who knew not only the specialized, but the generic, non-specialized resources of the community, and how to gain access to those as well. She wanted someone whose experience had taught them which alleys were blind alleys, so that she didn't need to waste her time on fruitless odysseys. She wanted a person who would level with her, even if it hurt a little; a counselor, but not in the psychotherapeutic sense. She needed someone who knew when to listen, who didn't sit in judgment, who would be loyal, especially during the hard times when we all act a little crazy. She wanted a person to whom she could confide her feelings of anger, of fear, of frustration, of despair. Above all, she wanted a friend.

THE CASE MANAGER AS FISCAL AGENT

By and large, it was parents who obtained the resources that today fund the programs serving their sons and daughters, and the paid staff who work in them. But while legislators and other public officials were deeply moved by the lobbying efforts of the parents, and felt charitably disposed toward them (after all, they knew it could be their own child), they nonetheless wanted assurances that someone would represent the interests of the other taxpayers, would serve as a good steward of the public trust, and would be a vigilant gatekeeper to the public coffers. They wanted case managers who would ask: "Is this person eligible under the law?" "Are the necessary eligibility documents properly completed and in the file?" "How do we know the money is being spent wisely?" "Are they really needy or could they find other ways to pay for the service?"

This characterization of public policymakers may make them appear mean-spirited or callous, but that isn't intended. Assuring maximally efficient use of tax dollars is their job, especially when we consider the number of people waiting for services. Toward that end, in some states the responsibility for provision of case management was placed under the welfare system, which has traditionally had a clear mandate to cut fraud or abuse. It is charged with operation of formal protective mechanisms to accomplish that oversight, including financial audits, licensing, certification, and rate setting of service providers, and establishing other regulatory mechanisms. Unfortunately, the world of public welfare, with its rules and regulations, is often unfamiliar to middle class citizens who never had to ask for help from the government, a problem which will be discussed.

THE CASE MANAGER AS SERVICE COORDINATOR

Many states are organized regionally or county-wide using specialized private or public agencies which are charged with responsibility for providing a full array of specialized services, e.g. residential, day programs, recreation, transportation, etc. In such agencies it is important for the administrators to coordinate the various parts of the delivery system to make them function as smoothly as possible, to have employees at the grass roots level who can be coordinating extensions of the administration. They also need someone to serve as a conduit, or clearinghouse, of information that should be shared with the different players, to orchestrate the work of the organization in order to avoid duplication of effort. The central concern in this role is efficient management and good control of the program. The appeal of setting up case management was that it seemed to be a logical way of achieving such efficiency and control.

Concern about coordination is not new. For instance, from 1947 until 1968 the United Fund of St. Paul, Minnesota and the Wilder Foundation produced a classic study which emanated from research on "multi-problem families" (Birt, 1956). These were families whose members were in contact with innumerable social service agencies, without the various agencies' awareness of the others' existence.

The appeal of this coordinating role has spread beyond the field of developmental disabilities. An increasing number of non-developmental-disability-specific organizations have adopted the service coordination role, and employ people called *case managers* to perform that function. Mental health programs, many vocational rehabilitation agencies, schools, public health departments and even self-contained institutions have begun to employ staff who are called *case managers*. However, such programs are usually not concerned with coordination over a life span, nor even coordination between their agency and other social service or generic agencies. Their focus is on coordination within their organization, and only during that period of the person's life that brings them into contact with the organization. Case Management for persons with developmental disabilities is often viewed as a life long role with the client and or family.

THE CASE MANAGER AS ENFORCER

Some advocates, particularly those familiar with the history of abuse and neglect of people with disabilities, believe that the pre-eminent function of case management should be to monitor, to provide vigorous advocacy, to assure that rights are protected, and bring sanctions to bear on wrong-doers if necessary. This role is almost a mix between "Robo-Cop," an indestructible defender of the literal interpretation of laws, and Clarence Darrow, who was skilled at finding the proper "fit" between the law's interpretation and the needs of his client. The case manager is expected to be knowledgeable in all applicable rules and regulations. The case manager exercises power, has the authority to withhold funds or rescind purchase of service contracts with incompetent or recalcitrant providers. The case manager is also envisioned to be almost a Renaissance man or woman, with extensive experience and training in a wide range of subjects, e.g., adaptive technologies for people with physical disabilities including positioning or other techniques, positive learning strategies for individuals with challenging behaviors, supported employment, and other state of the art methodologies.

THE TERM

In 1981, I wrote the following:

> One does not "manage" human beings, one serves them, helps them or advises them. Wolfensberger and Kurtz have presented a cogent argument for the use of the term *management* in their book on *Management of the Family of the Mentally Retarded* (1969). However, they also note that several of their counterparts "...objected to the term *management* because of its authoritarian overtones." While understanding the importance of honesty, and the reality of the control relationship which exists between client and service provider, I remain concerned about the dependent, subordinate tone evoked by "manager" and the inferior-superior relationship it implies between persons with developmental disabilities, their families, and the service providers. I am also concerned about the potential for depersonalization, dehumanization, and social distance between server and served created by the use of a word like "case" as a synonym for "human being." (Skarnulis, 1981).

Bergman is right in his belief that the term case management is not an appropriate term. It suggests dependency and passivity rather than independence and empowerment. Neufeldt, has suggested that case managers should be agents: "Surely if hockey players and film stars can have agents who argue on their behalf to get the best deals, people could also use agents to guarantee their fights and interests." (Neufeldt, 1977) Agent, advisor, service coordinator.....any words would be an improvement over the current term. It needs to be replaced.

CASE LOAD SIZE

How many people should a case manager be expected to serve? This seemingly simple suggestion has been vigorously debated with no resolution on the horizon. The range seems to be from as few as 10, for the first few years' transition of institution residents in the closure of the Hissom Memorial Center in Oklahoma, to as many as 100 or more. Part of the complexity of coming up with an "ideal" number results from the number of variables that can influence the response:

1. Degree of independence of the person served.
2. Related disabilities, e.g., behavioral or medical.
3. Family strengths e.g., income or other funding (insurance), extended family involvement, ability of family to provide support, etc..
4. Agency resources.
5. Case manager skill, experience, education.
6. Availability of community resources.
7. Duration of the disability.
8. Intensity of involvement, e.g., critical periods (first identification, return from institutional placement, divorce or death in family, school leaving/transition, etc.) or stable periods.
9. Role expectations described above, e.g., single function or multiple.

Experience also teaches that some assumptions about size can be misleading. People who are seemingly more capable and have fewer or less severe disabilities sometimes require more support (at least initially) when they are emancipated from the family home or an institution than those who have more severe disabilities. They are no different in this regard than normal young adults who discover that their new-found freedoms can lead to trouble.

The "mix" of children and adults can be important. When serving children, the focus tends to be primarily on supporting the family so as to provide stability for the child, whereas adults may themselves be the "primary" consumer. Further, the way in which people behave in one environment may not always be an accurate indicator of how they behave in another. All of which reinforces the importance of intimacy, of understanding and familiarity with the unique needs of each child and adult to be served, the basic criterion that can define whether a case load size is to be viewed as manageable.

RESOURCE LIMITS

Each of the four role expectations, taken singly, is clearly legitimate, and can be argued to be an essential function that *someone* must perform. But what happens when the roles conflict, when even the most competent person can't balance the priorities? For example, when a parent or person with disabilities wants the case manager to accompany them to the school for an individual education plan meeting, and the case manager's supervisor is concerned about processing back-logged reimbursement requests. Who has the final say? Since it was most often the lobbying efforts of the parents that resulted in the appropriations which pay for case management, perhaps the parents should have their needs met first, but as Novak, et al. have pointed out, one of the main appeals to legislators and others was the cost containment function. Agencies providing case management services have struggled with these realities for the past decade or more.

One of the most soul wrenching struggles that is occurring, and gaining steam, is the question of what are we willing to provide, and at what price. Body transplants, and a variety of sophisticated surgical interventions, computer-assisted eye gaze technology, mobility and communication devices are all available.... .at a price. What will society be willing to pay?

THE WELFARE MODEL

Some family members and citizens with disabilities bitterly dislike having to be associated with welfare programs. They think needed services should be provided as a matter of right, and not charity, that they are honest people who have worked hard to avoid asking for help, that they understand the value of money as well as their fellow taxpayers and will not foolishly spend what they are given. In fact, some would argue that these families would spend less than is currently the case in bureaucracies. These people resent a system that they too often see as penny wise and pound foolish, that will pay inordinate sums to move people out of their own homes but will do nothing to maintain them in those homes, that limits people to goods and services which have a medical *imprimatur* on them costing far more than readily available generic substitutes, that forces people to use expensive services provided by highly regulated professionals and specialized agencies rather than using neighbors, friends, or relatives. They dislike the broad brush of suspicion that has become endemic to the welfare system, where people are often viewed by the rest of society as essentially dishonest. They find welfare to be punitive, dehumanizing, and degrading. While one can legitimately protest that the dehumanization which permeates our welfare system is equally damaging to all of those who have to use it, and that what is needed is a societal attitude change to help *all* recipients, such observations, however true, do little to mollify parents and people with disabilities.

And the anger cuts both ways. It is very hard for a caring social worker to make a home visit in the suburbs, with manicured lawns and hot tubs on the decks, and then have to drive into the world of people who are bereft of the basic necessities of life. Parents of people with developmental disabilities have been remarkably successful at obtaining resources through legislative or judicial intervention. They assume that other devalued groups will admire and respect those gains, perhaps even model their own strategies after the successes of developmental disabilities. Wrong. Advocates for other groups, and often welfare staff members themselves, often resent those gains and what they believe to be a disproportionate share of resources targeted for those with developmental disabilities. Some welfare systems allow caseworkers to do their own priority setting, which makes balancing mixed caseloads of clients with a variety of problems more tolerable, but often results in short shrift for parents of people with disabilities because the worker serves others on the case load who are seen as more needy.

SOCIAL WORK AND CASE MANAGEMENT

In the preceding paragraph I used the term "social worker" and "caseworker" rather than case manager. Many social workers do not like being called case managers. Any professionally trained social workers would argue that their early leaders, such as Jane Adams and Dorothea Dix, personified many of the qualities now attributed to the case management role. They complain that if they had reasonable caseloads, reduced paper work, etc., that good social work would be what case management claims to be. Perhaps. But of course one of the reasons that advocates in developmental disabilities chose not to employ social workers, but to develop a new profession, was because mainstream social work agencies had not embraced developmental disabilities as a field in which to practice. Schools of social work provide little or no emphasis on developmental disabilities.

There were other concerns. Parents of children or adults with disabilities have great difficulty leaving home with them. Especially if the person has severe physical or behavioral problems, it is frequently impossible to obtain respite care in order for the parent to travel to an agency office. While there are exceptions, too often the traditional social service agency staff expected the parents to come to their office or they would not make home visits at night or on weekends when both parents could be present. During the 1940's and 1950's much of the social work literature relating to parents of children with mental retardation was preoccupied with a psychoanalytic interpretation of the problem, with heavy emphasis on the parents as "victims," as people suffering from severe psychopathology, rather than as people who weren't overcome so much with feelings of guilt or mourning as people who were physically exhausted and exasperated in their efforts to obtain services for their child. What parents didn't want was counselling or therapy. They wanted concrete help. Finally, their negative experiences with institution social workers who, like other professionals, advocated putting the child away, and with non-responsive community social service agencies, made them determined to create the kind of professional Betty Pendler described, and they were convinced it would have to be totally new.

If that perception is to change, and if the profession of social work, or any other profession, truly wants to produce case managers in developmental disabilities, it will need to begin by providing evidence of that desire. At a minimum it must acknowledge that the field of developmental disabilities is far more sophisticated than when it was based on a purely medical/institutional frame of reference. It must also include developmental disabilities training in its curriculum. Such training will need to explain what developmental disabilities are, address underlying values of contemporary service delivery, e.g., normalization and its corollaries (integration, age appropriateness, etc.), and will need to look at current adaptive communication and mobility technologies, as well as teaching strategies such as functional, community-referenced instruction based on an individual focussed, progressive service system. Beyond that, the field work placement for case managers needs to be in the non-specialized world of real jobs, real homes, real schools, and real community. They must learn how to broker services and gain entry into the community-at-large.

THE STRUCTURE OF THE ORGANIZATION

There are other examples of dissonance, of competing priorities, that seek resolution in years to come. When the consumers want the case manager to put on an advocacy hat, it is sometimes the same agency that employs the case manager which is the source of the problem. For example, while parents and individuals with disabilities expect the case manager to go outside the employer's "menu" of specialized, often segregated services, the case manager may be limited to providing only those goods and services which the agency delivers. Case managers have been instructed to not accept applications for services, or are prohibited from keeping waiting lists, because the sponsoring agency fears that information will be used by consumers as a presumption of entitlement.

Some organizations are legally limited by their charter to serve only certain populations, for example, only children. And so the family must seek a new provider each time their child leaves a category. Parents want continuity. They don't want to have to cycle through redundant intake procedures, giving the same identifying information every time, explaining the same reasons for requesting service, and hunting for the same bank statements, marriage licenses, birth certificates, again and again.

In the mid-1960's many Associations for Retarded Citizens decided to adopt a new policy, "to obtain, but not provide services." Their rationale was that if one delivers direct services, it may be difficult or impossible to monitor the quality or quantity of those services. Thus, they saw a conflict of interest between the role of advocate, monitor, and service provider. Yet many case management agencies also provide direct services. Why is there not a similar concern with conflict of interest? In truth there often is. But it is tough for case managers to fulfill the role of advocate, or whistle-blower, when the object of that action could be their own agency or fellow employees. Some case management agencies are organized so that the agency head has several divisions, one of which is case management. This administrative configuration, because of the separation of divisions, is felt to be an external, independent, case management system. Unfortunately, whenever the same employer signs the pay checks of employees such distinctions on the organization chart don't necessarily translate into the workplace. We have seen the so-called "conspiracy of silence" occur in large institutional settings, when employees who were aware of abuse or neglect were unwilling to report it because of pressure brought to bear by fellow employees. We do not need conditions which breed similar conspiracies in newly-developing community programs.

An important part of Medicaid reform has always been the requirement that case management services be provided by an external, independent agency. While governmental agencies have generally been viewed as in compliance with that requirement, experience indicates that local, county, and state employees who depend on their administrations for funding services are likely to let organizational allegiances influence their willingness to challenge their system.

It may be political naivete to believe that any entity could ever be totally free of untoward influences which interfere with advocacy on behalf of children and adults with developmental disabilities. However, some options seem at least worth considering. Agencies such as the protection and advocacy agencies formed under the Developmental Disabilities Act have generally been successful in separating themselves organizationally from direct service providers, including governmental entities, thus enabling them to effectively advocate and monitor. As noted above, some voluntary organizations, for example, some chapters of the Associations for Retarded Citizens, have maintained themselves as relatively pure advocacy agencies, not providing direct services. Further, some have broadened their mandate to serve *all* children and adults with developmental disabilities. Perhaps case management should be provided by an organization like one of these, or even sub-contracted through those agencies to a totally separate entity?

A word of caution is in order, however. The skills of a good case manager include the ability to negotiate, to mediate, and persuade. The world which they want people with disabilities to enter isn't the specialized world of disability, but the one which the majority of people experience. That requires a different brief, or mandate, for a case manager than one which limits contacts to the disability culture. If case managers are to serve as integration facilitators, they need to have a much different bag of tricks than the ones commonly found in case management training programs. The real world does not understand the jargon of developmental disabilities. You don't make friends with threats of lawsuits. You can't force people to be friends. The enforcer role has limited utility outside specialized agencies.

If what is at the root of our disenchantment with service systems is an absence of an appropriate sense of values about, and a respect for, basic human dignity, or a systemic inability to actualize such values, then litigation is a clumsy tool. The legal process may be able to force people *to act as if they care,* but it cannot actually get them to care, and that makes all the difference (Sundram, 1989).

CONSUMER CASE MANAGEMENT AND VOUCHERS

As Zirpoli, Wieck, and McBride point out, some parents who have had competency based training are very often capable of relieving case managers of some of their responsibilities, freeing the managers to focus on the needs of others. Case management is not the center of the universe around which all other services revolve. The center of the universe is reserved for the child or adult with a disability. Case management is simply one of many services which may be needed, like schooling, or work, an option which consumers should be able to use or not use. Ideally, they should be able to choose the case manager and agency as well, with degrees of case management involvement, agreed upon in advance by the person with disabilities, the parents or guardian, and the case management agency, and with opportunities for review at regular intervals. We live in a pluralistic society, with racial, cultural, and lifestyle preferences leading us in our choice making. Selection of a case manager should allow such pluralism. Ultimately, of course, whether case management is considered successful or not depends on whether it meets the needs of the person being served, rather than how it's done, or by whom.

While it is true that governmental entities may feel uncomfortable with the prospect of turning over resources and authority to the recipients of public funds, and will want safeguards for their use, there are compelling arguments for dividing up the tasks of case managers and considering relinquishing some of them to the consumers. Whether to protect consumers, or to control costs, well intentioned efforts often result in the opposite outcome. Experience has demonstrated that in many instances the protections are more costly, and burdensome, than what the consumers would have arranged if left to their own devices. As noted earlier, parents often want less expensive services than those given, are frequently appalled when they learn how much their child's programs cost, and realize how easily they could have met their needs with a little creativity and less money. They are acutely aware of the waiting lists, often having experienced them first hand, and want others to get help as well.

It really is true that the time has long passed for serious consideration to be given to a national voucher system. Wray, in this volume, does an excellent job of outlining the problems in the current funding mechanisms and the need for increased empowerment, at the individual level, of consumers and case managers. It has become almost axiomatic that every time services or goods get called "special" they cost more, segregate more, and isolate more. An analysis of family subsidy programs in the states that have them reveals that people with disabilities, and their advocates, have been very good at finding ways to keep costs down. Conversely, bureaucracies have a long history of being less than sagacious shoppers, enough to keep state attorney generals and the federal General Accounting Office happily employed. Nor have the professional architects of programs, armed with concepts like economies of scale and critical mass specialization, distinguished themselves by their ability to control costs. It really is time to replace top-down systems decision making with an individual-up model. Whether in the Pentagon or human services, the history of consumer spending and value received, reflects credit on the consumers rather than the reverse. If abuses of trust occur, increased oversight can always be provided.

SUMMARY

Athletes often find that by focusing their mental energy on imaging what they will be doing in a particular event, step by step, they can improve their performance. This concept, called "imaging" reflects an active attempt to influence the future (Furlong, 1979). The previous chapters have identified both the strengths and weaknesses of case management practice in the United States and Canada. What is needed now is to begin building consensus on what the vision of case management (or whatever it will be called) is to be and begin "imaging" the steps required to create the kind of future people with disabilities and their families want and deserve.

> "You can get a lot with a smile. You can get more with a smile and a gun" (Al Capone).

Consumers have smiled. Increasingly their "gun" has been knowledge. The past decade or more has seen the emergence of a new breed of parent-professionals and primary consumers who have knowledge, and as a result, power. The veteran parent-professionals—Elizabeth Boggs, Ann and Rudd Turnbull, Allan Bergman, Fran Smith, Dolores Norley, Eleanor Elkin, Bob McDonald, Betty Pendler, and others, are being joined by newly-empowered young parents and people with disabilities. They are members and graduates of programs like Partners in Policymaking and People First. They are determined to make a difference. They will insist on being part of the consensus building process. They were the hope in the past and perhaps more than any other single element, they constitute the hope for the future.

References

Blanck, P.D. and Turner, A.N. (1987). Organizational behavior and methodologies. *Handbook of Organizational Behavior.* New York: Prentice-Hall.

Furlong, W.B. (1979). The power of imagination. *Quest.* Washington, D.C.

Governor's Citizens' Committee on Mental Retardation. (1968). The report of the Nebraska Citizens' Study Committee on Mental Retardation. Vol. 1. Lincoln, NE. State Department of public institutions.

Neufeldt, A.H. (1977). Coordination simply stated. *Mental Retardation*. Canadian Association for the Mentally Retarded.

Skarnulis, E. (1981). Case management functions within the context of a comprehensive service system: where do they fit? *National Conference on Social Welfare - Final Report*. Washington, D.C. Administration on Developmental Disabilities, U.S. Department of Health and Human Services.

Sundram, C. J. (1989). Advocacy: To What Should We Aspire? *Quality of Care Newsletter*. Albany, New York. New York State Commission on Quality of Care.

CHAPTER XII

A New Way of Thinking for Case Managers

by Colleen Wieck

Over the past several years, we have learned about people with developmental disabilities, what they are capable of doing, what is important in their lives, and how they can be supported in communities. Lippert (1986) has listed seven changes that have occurred in the 1980s:

- A shift from expanding system capacity to increasing services quality. This does not mean all people have been served. It means advocates must argue for both capacity and quality.
- A move from fixed and predetermined expectations of persons with severe disabilities to higher and more demanding expectations by the individuals themselves, their families, and service providers.
- A move from short-term, developmental planning to life-long, functional planning.
- A move from providing a service continuum with emphasis on "special facilities and programs" to seeking a service array that adapts generic resources by providing the assistance and support as needed.
- A move from a fragmented grouping of separate and independent services (residential, day training, education) to recognition of the need for a holistic, interdependent and integrated service system.
- A move from a system of offering models of service delivery to one where it is possible to create individualized support.
- A move from service payment based on facility budgets toward reimbursement based on vendor performance and individual needs.

There are several implications of these changes for case managers.

The Association for Retarded Citizens—United States (1987) recently released a study of waiting lists. A conservative estimate is that 250,000 individuals are waiting for community services. Case managers are at the battle line between people in need and a lack of resources. The shift that has occurred no longer allows case managers to accept any service or an inappropriate service.

Expectations are changing as a result of better methods of teaching and adaptations that can be made to the settings. People can learn regardless of severity of disability with the right types and amount of supports.

The changes in planning approaches reflect the shift away from developmental assessments, curricula, and evaluation approaches to an approach that recognizes people a need to learn skills necessary to live and work as adults.

The shift to an array of supports means that people with disabilities are no longer referred and placed waiting to move through a continuum of services. Case managers must now broker services, often relying on support and generic agencies.

In the past, each type of service operated fairly independently. Now, case managers can pull the services together through a team and integrated approach of planning.

Case managers were accustomed to the latest model often linked with funding. For years, "model" of residential services was ICF-MR, the only variation was size. Now, there is a shift from models to creation of individualized, personalized services.

Because of the preceding shift, case managers are also faced with a change in how services are funded. Reimbursement is often linked with individuals rather than programs or facilities.

The New Way of Thinking Starts from a Different Perspective

People with developmental disabilities are, first and foremost, people with ability. Without special assistance, some people with developmental disabilities cannot take advantage of the freedoms and opportunities of our society. People with developmental disabilities have special needs, but their basic needs are the same. Funding, policies, and services often have been focused only at the special needs of people with developmental disabilities. The result has been that their basic needs have gone unmet.

We have learned that services are most successful when basic needs are met in the context of addressing special needs.

Case managers are responsible for gently reminding providers and policy makers that people with developmental disabilities, like all people, need:

- To be seen, first of all, as people.
- To experience love and friendship.
- To experience continuity in their lives, especially in relation to the people who are important to them.
- To be respected and treated with dignity.

- To have access to opportunities and information, to make choices and to exercise their rights.
- To have a decent and appropriate place to live.
- To have meaningful employment and contribute to the community.
- To have opportunities to continue to learn throughout their lives.

In response to these basic needs, there are four basic issues—having a home, not just a roof over our heads; learning skills which are useful to our lives and careers, not just going to school; working, not just keeping busy; and developing and sustaining relationships with people who depend on us and upon whom we can depend.

A real home is a place to live the most personal moments of our lives. A home provides security and comfort, allows us to make choices and express ourselves. The people who share our homes are usually the people with whom we choose to spend time, be ourselves, and feel close.

Real learning is lifelong. It means learning to understand ourselves. Learning involves developing skills which are useful to us both as individuals and as members of communities. The people with whom we learn are also teachers. Many become friends we can count on throughout our lives.

Real work means earning a living, being productive, and making a contribution to our community.

Having a real friend means being involved with someone who chooses to spend time with you just because they want to and not because they are paid to do so. Real friends broaden our opportunities and enrich our lives. Real friends are hard to find. It takes most of us a long time through contact with many different people to find that small group of friends who really matter. Friendships are essential.

People with developmental disabilities often are more handicapped by the environment than by their disabilities. Historically, our thinking and actions have focused on the inabilities of people with developmental disabilities. The concern was with "fixing the person" or "curing the deficit." Over time, that focus has shifted to building on capabilities and assisting individuals to develop and use their abilities.

The most dramatic shift in our way of thinking is the recognition that the social and physical environments are often a greater issue than abilities and disabilities. This is especially true in considering the expectations others have of people with developmental disabilities, and what people do based on those expectations.

We have made great advances in bringing very sophisticated technology to bear on the lives of people with disabilities. People who have trouble speaking were often unable to interact with others because of the low level of technology put at their disposal. People who had trouble moving their hands simply could not use sign language to their advantage. In a very short period of time, we have moved from manual spelling boards to laptop computers to Synthesized speech to gaze-activated computers.

The new way of thinking about developmental disabilities emphasizes supporting individuals, families, and communities. Case managers often recognize that support has several dimensions:

- Basing the Provision of services on the informed choices, strengths, and needs of individuals with developmental disabilities and their families, rather than forcing them to choose among a narrow range of pre-set options and approaches.
- Planning and providing services based on what people need and the abilities they have, rather than providing more services than are needed, or not providing those services which are needed.
- Supporting the individual, family, and community members to gain access to the resources available in the community jobs, houses, relationships with families, friends, and associates— rather than replacing those resources with places populated only by professionals and other people with disabilities.
- Coordinating services and supports around the life of the individual rather than around the needs of staff and services.
- Recognizing the abilities of ordinary citizens-children, coworkers, neighbors—to teach people skills, assist them to participate and contribute, model appropriate behaviors, and develop relationships.

A New Way of Learning

In our society, learning is a valued activity, important to the development of individuals. Many citizens with developmental disabilities have difficulty learning. It is critical that we develop strategies and approaches to prepare children for life and enhance their individual capabilities.

Historically, the changes in our thinking about education have paralleled, and in some cases determined, our thinking about other areas of life. When the institutional approach prevailed, young people with developmentaj disabilities did not attend public schools. They stayed at home; were admitted to state institutions; or attended special, private schools.

Federal legislation (P.L. 94-142), passed in 1975, shifted emphasis from one of getting children with disabilities into schools to an emphasis on the nature of the education they receive. Federal education policy supported the concept of individualized, outcome-oriented learning experiences for all children with disabilities. Case managers need to be familiar with several educational concepts such as:

FREE AND APPROPRIATE EDUCATION. Public schools must identify all students with disabilities within their geographic areas and provide free instructional and support services to meet each student's unique educational needs.

INDIVIDUALIZED. Public schools must recognize that each learner is unique and has a right to an education which is tailored to individual strengths and needs.

INTEGRATED SETTINGS. To the maximum extent appropriate, children with disabilities are to be educated with children who are not disabled. Unfortunately, the choice used to be if you wanted to learn something, you had to be in a segregated class. Now parents are saying, "We want integrated settings"—regardless of the development of excellent skills which may be worthless in the real world.

DUE PROCESS. Parents or guardians must be provided with prior written notice of actions which might affect the status of their child.

The first generation of students served by P.L. 94-142 are now graduating, and their parents have higher expectations than earlier generations of parents. Case managers must be ready for this new generation. It is unlikely that parents and caregivers who have invested heavily in children's services will be satisfied with an adult service system that can only produce a 20 percent employment level or a service system in which 80 percent of the recipients will be living below the poverty line one year after separation from high school (Fifield and Smith, 1985). Case managers will be expected to assist in brokering services that match educational concepts of least restrictive, age-appropriate, and functional.

There is considerable knowledge about what is required to plan, implement, and evaluate an individualized and functionally oriented education for students with disabilities. This new way of thinking about learning and belonging is well articulated. The following examples identify some of the components of a quality education based in part on criteria described by Donnellan (1986). Case managers can use this same set of criteria to review individual plans for their clients and during monitoring visits.

The Content, Style, People, Objectives, and Places of Education Must be Age Appropriate and Individualized

Students with developmental disabilities often cannot learn all of the skills which can be learned by nonhandicapped people of the same age. At the same time, it is inappropriate to offer programs which are geared to significantly younger students. The goal is to minimize the differences in performance of people with developmental disabilities and their peers. Instructional materials, peer interactions, learning objectives, and services locations all must be chronologi cally age-appropriate, Young adults do not play with wooden puzzles or sing nursery rhymes.

Case managers should be alert for age-appropriate materials during site visits. In our state, a staff attorney found the following items during a site visit for young adult programming:

> Kitty puppy puzzle; Fat Albert puzzle; Candyland—a child's first toy; and Ring toss (Granquist, personal communication, 1986).

THE GOALS, OBJECTIVES AND ACTIVITIES OF EDUCATION MUST BE FUNCTIONAL

People with developmental disabilities need to learn things that are truly useful to them. The functional aspects of skills related to working, for instance, can be assessed by asking, "Would someone be paid to do this?" People do not get paid to stack rings or match colors. As an example, students could be taught to sort knives, forks, and spoons instead of learning to sort colored tiles. Case managers should assess the functional nature of individual programs.

INTERACTIONS WITH NONHANDICAPPED PEERS AND OTHERS ARE ESSENTIAL

The Education for All Handicapped Children Act (P.L. 94-142) requires that students be educated with nonhandicapped students to the "maximum extent appropriate. It is not only appropriate, but essential to ensure that people with developmental disabilities have a wide variety of opportunities to interact with peers and others who are not disabled. Education should involve a variety of such opportunities at school and away from school. The more constructive, comprehensive and long lasting the interactions the better—the development of mutual respect and interest takes time. Case managers need to assist in the development of friendships by assuring opportunities for interaction with nonhandicapped peers.

A VARIETY OF PEOPLE AND INSTRUCTIONAL ARRANGEMENTS NEED TO BE INVOLVED

People with developmental disabilities need to learn how to interact with people other than teachers and how to use skills in a variety of settings. This means that activities should be designed to enable interaction with a wide variety of people. Programs which facilitate learning functional skills in a variety of environments are more appropriate than programs which confine learning to single environments. People learn skills best in the natural places where they happen. For example, bedmaking should be taught in the home and grooming should be taught in the locker room or a dressing room, not a classroom. Case managers can offer the coordination between settings to assure that skills are taught in the appropriate settings

HIGHLY INDIVIDUALIZED ADAPTATIONS MUST BE MADE

Many students with developmental disabilities will not be able to participate in a variety of situations and environments unless specialized and individualized adaptations are made. These adaptations include alternate ways of communicating, changing the order in which things are accomplished, and modifying the setting. A person learning to read who is unable to turn the pages should be provided with a page turning device. Case managers do not have to be experts in all aspects of technology, but they should be familiar with resources that can assess and prescribe assistive devices.

PREPARING FOR THE FUTURE IS CRITICAL

Parents and educators need to focus on how and where the student will function as an adult and gear learning activities toward the actual work and living arrangement the person will experience. Students with disabilities who will live on their own must learn cooking, shopping, and other skills leading to self-reliance. Case managers will be one of the key resources during the transition process from public schools to adult services. The outcome of living and working in the community is the ultimate criterion.

A New Way of Living

Throughout the United States and Canada, there is a growing recognition that having a real home is as important to people with developmental disabilities as it is for everyone else. For children, home means parents or guardians who build an atmosphere of love, affection, security, and comfort. For all of us, home means moral and material security and a place to invite friends.

The gradual recognition that real homes are important to people with developmental disabilities has led to significant policy shifts in residential services including:

- Efforts to reduce the numbers of people with developmental disabilities in state institutions and to increase the resources available for community options.
- Efforts to increase the support available to individuals and families so people with developmental disabilities can maintain their homes in the community.

RETURNING PEOPLE TO COMMUNITIES

The trend toward deinstitutionalization began in the 1960s. Prior to that time, the prevailing practice was to admit both children and adults with developmental disabilities to state institutions on an indefinite basis. Over the last 15 years, efforts have focused on preventing out-of-home placement and moving children from institutions to less restrictive settings. The

)f-home placement in the United States had risen from
;0s to 21 years in 1985. Between 1977 and 1982, there
iildren (birth to 21 years) in out-of-home placements.
2s have contributed to the shift from an institutional
___uing residential care to a community approach:

- Litigation in several states established the right to treatment and placement in the least restrictive environment. The population of state institutions continues to drop every year from a national high of 195,000 in 1967 to under 100,000 today.
- Title XIX or Medicaid funds (1971) stimulated the development of ICF-MR faciltiies in the community.
- The Education for All Handicapped Children Act (P.L. 94-142) has had a dramatic effect on reducing the number of children with developmental disabilities in out-of-home placements. P.L. 94-142 guaranteed the right of all children with disabilities to receive an education. It also enabled families to be relieved of responsibilities during the day, thus assisting them to better support their children at home.

The individual approach to services in the community reflects a newer and still developing way of thinking about where people with developmental disabilities live. The emphasis is on promoting desirable outcomes through individualized planning and case management. The goal is not to "make a placement," but rather to flexibly design and manage a variety of settings and resources which will support the development of a real home. The emphasis is on using typical residential settings. Needed support might be minor or major and involve one or more of the following: a daily phone call or regular visit to the home, an access ramp or bathlift, special training for parents, periodic respite, or a live-in roommate or care provider. These supports are important and often critical. They do not, however, alter the desirable characteristics of a "home." Case managers must be familiar with the array of services funded in their particular state. With the Title XIX Home and Community BasedWaiver, case managers must be able to broker services needed to support the individual in a regular home.

The Home and Community Based Waiver waives Medicaid regulations to encourage people to leave ICF-MR facilities and to prevent people from being placed out of the home into these facilities. Services involve case management, respite care, homemaker and in-home support services, supported living arrangements, day habilitation, and minor adaptations to a house or apartment.

In order to qualify for waivered services, a person must: (I) have a diagnosed developmental disability; (2) be eligible for Medicaid; (3) be a resident of an ICF-MR facility or at risk of becoming a resident within one year if community support is not provided; and (4) have planned and documented needs for daily intervention.

Another type of individualized approach is the family subsidy program cash grant to families to cover a portion of expenses for diagnostic assessment, homemaker services, training, special equipment, visiting nurses, therapists, preschool programs, related transportation, and/or parental relief or child care. Most state-funded programs are intended to assist families to maintain their children with developmental disabilities at home. Case managers often work with families to secure family subsidy or family support.

The reality is that less than 1 percent of all residential funds are used to support families—the people most often involved in providing a real home for people with developmental disabilities.

At the same time facilities and smaller community options have developed in Minnesota, we also have had increased experience with different ways of organizing the delivery of services. The idea of supporting families so their children can stay at home was a major change in thinking. For adults, case managers may be asked to assist individuals in arranging consumer-owned housing which is a recent development in Canada, the northeastern United States, and other states. Families or individuals with developmental disabilities buy or rent housing, and receive support services. Because an individual has a home, it is the services that change as individual needs change. In some cases, substantial support is provided by neighbors. Formal services are involved in a supplemental way. The emphasis is on developing and supporting a home and neighborhood life for the individual by providing services as they are needed. Families have developed such arrangements for their sons and daughters. In Winnipeg, Canada, 60 people living in 20 households belong to the Prairie Housing Cooperative. Twelve of the sixty people have disabilities.

A New Way of Working

A staff person from an advocacy organization asked 20 children in a special education classroom, "What do you want to do when you grow up?" None of the children could answer the question. They had no idea what it meant to be a productive member of society.

We have changed our way of thinking about how people with developmental disabilities can become productive citizens and make contributions to their communities. We used to spend years preparing people with disabilities for eventual work or providing them with sheltered places in which to work. We have learned that by focusing on preparing people for work, we have often created circumstances that result in people never actually getting jobs. Today, we have learned that if we support individuals to find jobs, we can then quite effectively teach them the skills for that job and make adaptations to the work place that increase their ability to do the job. We can support people to work while training them on the job.

We have learned that if we assist people to find, obtain, and retain employment, there are significant benefits for the people as well as for society. The individuals earn a wage, have the opportunity to make a contribution to the community, are more able to learn from and develop relationships with nonhandicapped people, and have greater opportunities to exercise choice in their lives. The community, at the same time, derives the benefits of their work and relates with people who have disabilities as contributing citizens.

Employment is important to most citizens, and citizens with developmental disabilities are no exception. The unfortunate reality is that most of these citizens are not working. Lou Harris and Associates (1986) indicated that two-thirds of all Americans with disabilities between the ages of 16 and 64 are not working. One in four works full time, and another 10 percent work part time. Two-thirds of those who are not working said they would like to have a job.

Several agencies, communities, states, and the federal government are redesigning the way vocational and employment services are delivered to people with developmental disabilities. This change is most evident in the number of states receiving grants from the United States Department of Education Office of Special Education and Rehabilitative Services (OSERS) to establish statewide systems of supported employment opportunities for people with severe disabilities. On October 1, 1985, ten states were awarded grants; and on October 1, 1986, an additional seventeen states became involved. Over one-half of the states are now initiating changes from a system of sheltered employment and day activities to one based on supported employment.

Over the last two decades, there have been two distinct types of developments in community services related to work and employment—the early development of facilities to provide rehabilitation and sheltered employment programs. Changes in the federal Rehabilitation Act and other legislation have reflected historical developments in each of these areas.

The 1986 amendments to the Rehabilitation Act acknowledge the new way of working. Case managers should be aware of three important elements in this Act:

- Supported employment is recognized as an acceptable outcome for employability. Supported employment is defined as employment in an integrated setting for individuals with severe disabilities for whom such employment has not traditionally occurred.
- Severe disability is defined in terms of functioning level and extent of services required rather than a diagnostic label.
- Rehabilitation engineering is recognized as a component of vocational rehabilitation.

Supported employment programs provide intensive, ongoing services required by people who are unable to secure and maintain competitive employment. The intent is to provide long-term support, or support as long as it is needed.

Supported employment means paid work in a variety of integrated settings, particularly regular work sites, especially designed for severely handicapped individuals, irrespective of age or vocational potential for: (1) people for whom competitive employment at or above minimum wage traditionally has not been available; and (2) people who, because of disability, need intensive ongoing postemployment support to perform in the work setting.

Supported employment is further outlined in OSERS guidelines which specify the minimum criteria as:

- At least 20 hours of paid work per week;
- No more than eight persons with disabilities served at any one job site; and
- Ongoing publicly funded support.

These guidelines show how supported employment differs from traditional services. Traditional services focus on short-term assistance and training in order to produce long-term employment. For people who have the most severe disabilities, short-term support is not sufficient for obtaining and maintaining employment. Ongoing support can mean:

- Job analysis—matching individuals with jobs.
- Ongoing training—teaching social and work skills required on the job.
- Ongoing follow-along on the job for as long as required.
- Transportation.
- Ongoing support to the employer.

Case managers must be aware of the various types of ongoing support in brokering these services. For each individual, there may be variations in the amount of support provided over time, the degree of social and physical integration with nondisabled workers, and pay options.

Some of the effects of supported employment services identified by local providers include the following:

- As a result of the achievements made by people who have been placed, many professionals have changed their perceptions about what is possible.
- The retention rate in community job placement has been higher than expected.
- Community job placement typically has been accompanied by improvements in grooming posture and behavior.
- Community job placement has been accompanied by movement to less restrictive places to live (Kaliszewski, personal communication, 1986).

Impact of Developments

Increasingly, attention is shifting to a concern with real work for pay along side nondisabled people. The impact of higher expectations, innovative projects, conferences, and consultations is being felt. The system is progressing, but it has far to go in addressing: the underemployment, inappropriate employment, or complete unemployment of individuals with disabilities.

Certainly, the application of the supported employment approach is consistent with the new way of thinking about people with developmental disabilities. The momentum is building; and as we gain experience with this new way of creating opportunities, many issues are becoming clearer:

- Once again, funding regulations are often inconsistent with the more individualized approach. For instance, day programs are natural providers of supported employment programs; yet if Medicaid is a primary source of revenue for these programs, funding restrictions in the area of employment make leadership by these programs difficult.
- To make supported employment a permanent and integrated part of policy and practice, it should be included in state statute and funds should be allocated. To date, operational guidelines for supported employment have been determined by the terms and conditions of the federal OSERS grant and by recommendations in the professional literature.
- The change in both policy and practice from segregated work sites to more dispersed employment in integrated settings requires skills and values training for service organizations and staff, a different approach to monitoring, and support to the parents and guardians of people with developmental disabilities.

Recent Congressional action addressed fiscal disincentives for workers and is helping to build momentum for individualized employment support. Section 1619 of the Social Security Act was enacted as a three-year demonstration project effective January 1, 1981 (made permanent in 1986) to remove work disincentives for recipients of Supplemental Security Income (551) disability benefits who work despite continuing disabilities. Prior to enactment of Section 1619, recipients could lose eligibility for cash benefits and Medicaid coverage if they engaged in substantial, gainful activity. Section 1619 contains two basic provisions:

- Section (a) : Extension of cash and Medicaid benefits to individuals whose earnings prevent eligibility for regular 551 cash benefits (as income increases, cash benefits are reduced); and
- Section (b) Extension of Medicaid coverage to individuals whose earnings, although high enough to prevent eligibility for 551, are not high enough to cover medical care.

Case managers must be familiar with these Social Security Amendments to ensure individuals do receive waivers.

A New Way of Assessment, Planning, Implementation and Evaluation

A new way of thinking about education, living, and working in the community requires different approaches of assessment, planning, implementing, and evaluating services.

ASSESSMENTS

All of us have been trained to write assessments that tend to be very oriented to needs, deficits, problems, or negative statements. I can pick up a case record and read a summary of physical condition, family history, problems, diagnoses, what the person doesn't do in the developmental sequence, and then at the end, there are one or two sentences—Joe has a good sense of humor or Mary likes people.

Let us rethink this approach of assessments.

Every person who is employed has a performance appraisal at least once a year. Performance appraisals even for people we don't like tend to be fairly positive. We probably work our way through a performance appraisal making wonderful statements and then say, "Oh, by the way, could you please show up for work?" or "I don't want to mention it, could you please stop stealing from the company?" Perhaps to illustrate how very differently we describe people with disabilities compared to employees, mentors, or leaders in the field, the following case profile has been prepared for one of our national leaders. Our national leader is:

> Male, caucasian, who is overweight, has hypertension, is on a low calorie diet, is currently on eight medications, has occasional outbursts according to his family, and needs to control his temper tantrums according to staff.

> Our national leader enjoys eating and drinking coffee. He does not sleep well at night. (He slept through the entire night only 94 percent of the time during last month.)

> Staff report that he needs to be provided with activities to keep him busy, but he does have difficulty adjusting to change.

> He needs to have his hair cut short to prevent him from pulling it out.

> He needs help in choosing appropriate attire for social engagements.

When he thinks no one is watching, he entertains himself
by blowing fuzz balls around on his desk.

All of these statements are direct quotes from case records. Contrast this
profile with the typical glowing remarks we make about our national leaders.

The challenge is to assess a person's strengths and to write statements
that you would say about yourself or family members. Case managers need
to stop describing stacking, stringing, and pointing behaviors and substitute
functional approaches. After reading a profile, an outsider should be able to
describe what the person can do in the regular environment.

The challenge for case managers is to read literature about functional
assessment, listen to speakers, and experiment with a different approach to
assessment. Most family members will welcome a new way of assessment.

PLANNING

In the old days, we had one person in charge, usually a medical doctor who
would "pronounce" what would occur to individuals with disabilities. We
would refer to that person as God or Dr. God, depending upon personal
preference.

That approach to individual planning did not work because other
professionals also had an interest and perspective in the person's life. The
team was created, and the team grew and grew. Now we have the Cecil B.
De Mille approach to planning with thousands of people sitting around a
table, each with a part of a script to recite. After the entire script is read, the
spotlight goes on, and everyone turns to the end of the table where the
individual with disabilities and his/her family are sitting. The question
asked is "What do you think?" Many people report the sudden urge to leave.

The challenge to case managers who chair team meetings is to make the
team approach work without intimidating every individual and family. Can
the team meetings include people who are friends or have relationships with
the individual with a disability? Can case managers begin to use personal
futures planning approaches rather than preprinted scripts?

IMPLEMENTATION

At the forefront of the implementation are two words—respect and dignity.
During the past two decades, there have been several phases of special
education which did not provide respect and dignity. We never asked people
with disabilities what they needed or wanted. Instead, we tried several new
methodologies including:

- Operationalizing normalization through schedules which called
  for watered-down elementary school academics in the morning,
  music and crafts after lunch, bowling on Tuesdays, swimming on
  Thursdays, and birthdays celebrated once a month at the conven-
  ience of the Ladies Club.

- Gross motor phase which entailed balance beams, trampolines, parachute play, exercise mats, and individuals walking around with objects attached to their heads, hands, and feet to help them develop better coordination.
- Developmental model featuring hundreds of developmental scales and curricula that began with the assumption every individual must work through several steps from infants to toddlers to children to adulthood. Unfortunately, most people ended up never progressing past stacking blocks, stringing beads, and assembling puzzles.
- The behaviorism phase came in with a new vocabulary such as antecedents, consequate, precision teaching, stimulus, DRO, and overcorrection. The precision mentality was applied to developmental tasks yielding objectives such as, "Bill will shave 50 percent of his face with 70 percent accuracy on 3 of 14 consecutive days."

Case managers need to recognize that implementation has been revolutionized by a functional approach that is community referenced. Technology will create additional ways of augmenting the strengths and capacities of individuals to live and work in the community.

EVALUATION

At the top of the list on every individual plane should be friendships and relationships for individuals with disabilities—hopefully, the friends will be people who are not paid to be with this individual. In addition to the demand for friendships, case managers should be comfortable with the following criteria:

> Age-Appropriate: Would these materials be used by a nondisabled person of the same chronological age? Would these skills be performed by a nondisabled person of the same chronological age?

> Community Referenced: If objectives are met, will there be participation in a variety of integrated community settings? Are objectives meeting basic skills needed in the future?

> Functional: If the person does not learn skills described in the objective, will someone else have to do those activities? Do the activities involve mutual interaction with nondisabled peers?

> Generalization: Are skills taught or performed with natural cues and reinforcement? Are the skills taught in

the natural settings where they will need to be performed (home, community settings)?

Choice: Are the objectives based on a comprehensive assessment that emphasizes strengths of the individual? Do the objectives reflect individual's choices and interests? Do the objectives reflect family's choices and interests?

Case managers are absolutely critical to the conversion from traditional services to community integration. Case managers should not accept special buildings as community integrated settings. People with disabilities can live, work, and play in regular houses, work sites, and recreational areas. Case managers should also not assume individuals with the most severe disabilities "need" the most restrictive settings. People with the most severe disabilities are living, working, and enjoying life in the least restrictive settings in several states and provinces.

Biographical Sketches

Angela Novak Amado, Ph.D., has published, researched, and trained others regarding community integration for all persons. She is currently a consultant regarding community services with the Human Services Support Network of St. Paul, Minnesota.

Luther A. Granquist is an attorney with Legal Advocacy for Persons with Developmental Disabilities in Minnesota. He has represented persons with developmental disabilities since 1972.

Mary Hubbard Linz is currently the Associate Director of Training for the Minnesota University Affiliated Program on Developmental Disabilities. She has worked in state and public school agencies in administrative and teaching positions over the past 24 years. Dr. Linz holds a doctorate in Special Education Administration from the University of Minnesota.

Dorothy Kerzner Lipsky is Senior Research Scientist, The Graduate School and University Center, The City University of New York. She has been an administrator in general and special education. In 1987-88, she was a Switzer Distinguished Fellow of the National Institute on Disability and Rehabilitation Research and currently she is serving as Project Director of an SSA-funded program serving youth with severe disabilities to assist in their transition from school to work. She is widely published, most recently as coeditor (with Alan Gartner), *Beyond Separate Education: Quality Education for All* (Brookes, 1989).

Patricia L. McAnally, former Associate Director of Training for the Minnesota University Affiliated Program on Developmental Disabilities, currently serves as a State Department of Education consultant in the area of hearing impaired. She has had extensive administrative, research, and teaching experience, and holds a doctorate in special education from the University of Minnesota.

Robert McDonald and his wife Judy Friend are the parents of three young children, two of whom have special needs. Bob is a former journalist with the Canadian Broadcasting Corporation and past president of the Gateway Association for the Mentally Handicapped in Edmonton, Alberta. He and his family now reside in Kingston, Ontario, where he is District Coordinator for the Resource, Educational and Advocacy Centre for the Handicapped (REACH).

Betty Pendler is the mother of two children, Lisa and Paul. Lisa has resided in a community residence for the past eight years, and Paul is a doctoral student in psychology. Ms. Pendler holds a master's degree in Community Health Education and is a consultant in the field of developmental disabilities. She has given workshops in the area of parent advocacy, staff training on understanding parents "letting go", sexuality, community living, and parent-professional relationships.

Carla A. Peterson has over 15 years experience in the field of early childhood education and intervention. Currently she is coordinating two research and evaluation projects for the Department of Educational Psychology at the University of Minnesota. Both projects involve working with young children and families, as well as professionals. Ms. Peterson has also held administrative and teaching positions in early childhood special education, child care and Head Start.

Edward R. Skarnulis, Ph.D., does research and consulting in the field of developmental disabilities. For the past ten years, he has been a state director of developmental disabilities services. Dr. Skarnulis has administered residential services and supervised case management. Dr. Skarnulis' doctorate is from the University of Nebraska.

Colleen Wieck is currently the Executive Director of the Governor's Planning Council on Developmental Disabilities for the State of Minnesota. She has had extensive experience as a planner, consultant, and administrator in the area of developmental disabilities. Dr. Wieck holds a doctorate in educational psychology from the University of Minnesota.

Lyle Wray is currently County Administrator for Dakota County, Minnesota. He served as Federal Court Monitor for the *Welsch* Consent Decree concerning services for persons with disabilities. He also served as Provincial Director of Mental Retardation Services for Newfoundland, Canada.